HOW TO OPEN AND OPERATE
A HOME-BASED
CATERING BUSINESS

HOW TO OPEN AND OPERATE A HOME-BASED CATERING BUSINESS

by Denise Vivaldo

Old Saybrook, Connecticut

Cover and text illustrations by Kathy Michalove

"How to Write a Press Release for Pickup" on pp. 116–17 by Jill Sandin, president/owner, Sandin Communications.

Library of Congress Cataloging-in-Publication Data

Vivaldo, Denise.
  How to open and operate a home-based catering business / Denise Vivaldo.
    p.   cm.
  ISBN 1-56440-240-1
  1. Caterers and catering   I. Title
TX911.2.V58   1993
641'.4—dc20   93-22782
                                                        CIP

Manufactured in the United States of America
First Edition/Fifth Printing

To Louie and John

Contents

Acknowledgments

There were days when I was writing this book that I felt I would never get to the end. I discovered putting my knowledge on paper required a lot of discipline, dedication, and personal motivation. During the moments that I possessed none of these traits, I was lucky enough to have a support system of people to pull, drag, and push me forward to the last page.

My thank-yous start with Betsy Amster, series editor for Globe Pequot Press. Waging the war on unnecessary words, the woman is a general. Betsy extracted this book from all the extra pages I wrote. A mighty fine job she did, and I am in awe of her determination.

Next I need to thank Kit Snedaker, not only for her skill and her suggestions on this book but more importantly for the years she has listened to everything else I wrote and, no matter how awful the pages were, encouraged me to keep on writing.

I'd like to thank Laura Strom, acquisitions editor, and everyone else who works behind the scenes at Globe Pequot. I'm amazed at the amount of talent, energy, and people it takes to publish one book.

Last but not least, thank you to my husband, Ken Meyer, and my sister, Joan Vivaldo, two firstborns who enrich my life with their love and support. The two of them have taught me to keep my eye on the ball, always eat dessert first, and not be afraid to ask for what I want.

1
So You Think
You Want to Be a Caterer?

One night as dinner guests were leaving after another spectacular party, I thought, I should get paid for doing this! The next day I made some phone calls from the real estate office where I worked to see how I could realize my dream of becoming a caterer. A year later I was cooking foods I loved to fix and learning how to make catering my full-time job. Now ten years and thousands of parties later, I'm a home-based caterer. On average I direct five or six events each month, parties ranging from a fund-raiser for several thousand guests on a Hollywood sound stage to a wedding reception for one hundred guests in someone's backyard.

I also work with people who want to start their own catering business, and I train other caterers who want to expand. My services include recipe and menu development, public relations and promotional events, marketing brochures and portfolio design, as well as custom-tailored programs designed to solve my clients' problems.

For the last five years, I've taught catering courses up and

down the West Coast to men and women who want to entertain—people just like you. Like you, my students read cookbooks
and food magazines the way other people read newspapers. I'll
bet you buy every new kitchen gadget on the market. Chances
are you're already throwing parties for friends, colleagues, and
family without getting paid for it. You may even have gone so
far as to investigate cooking schools. Bravo! You're well on your
way to becoming a caterer.

Of course becoming a caterer doesn't happen overnight. As
we'll discuss, if you want firsthand experience, the best thing to
do is apprentice with another caterer or go to a cooking school.
You will also need to learn the nuts and bolts of running a catering business. That's where this book comes in. Follow the suggestions outlined here and learn how to

- set up your home office
- learn to be "the boss"
- write a business plan
- charge for your talent
- bid for and close deals
- write a proposal
- ask for deposit money up front
- package your own press kit
- put together a winning team of employees
- hire entertainers and musicians
- design the menu for a perfect party
- find new clients by referrals
- deal with elements beyond your control
- profit from every opportunity
- make money at something you love to do

Do You Have What It Takes?

As much fun as it is to cook and to give wonderful parties, catering is not for everyone. To evaluate your experience, motivation,
and interest in this business, look at the following questions. If
you can answer "yes" to most of them, you too can be a caterer.

- ☐ Do you have basic cooking skills?
- ☐ Do you have a working knowledge of food preparation and menu planning?
- ☐ Do you enjoy serving people, making them feel comfortable and at ease?
- ☐ Do you like to solve problems?
- ☐ Are you creative and resourceful?
- ☐ When you read a recipe, can you "taste" the finished dish before you even begin?
- ☐ Are you comfortable enough in the kitchen to cook without recipes?
- ☐ Do you dine out often and like different kinds of food?
- ☐ Are you gracious and polite in stressful situations?
- ☐ Are you good with a budget?
- ☐ Do you have money set aside to start a new business?
- ☐ Have you ever worked in sales?
- ☐ Will you be comfortable promoting yourself?
- ☐ Are you willing to leave your current career behind and start all over again as a caterer?

Opportunities in Catering

Hotels, country clubs, restaurants, charter yachts, even airlines—all represent catering opportunities; or you can create your own catering opportunities by "chefing" in private homes or executive dining rooms, directing catering for department stores, or supervising takeout counters in supermarkets. One way to jumpstart your new career is to contact an existing food purveyor and offer a specific item you'd like to sell—mocha-chip chocolate cookies, for instance.

Hotels

Most hotels have a separate catering division to handle banquet rooms. Entry-level positions, which are frequently available, may give you a chance to meet local clientele and thus build a client base of your own. You can also get a close look at how in-house catering works, and you might discover some service you alone can provide.

When hotels rent out banquet rooms to outside caterers for a party, they usually let the caterer use the hotel kitchen. I got to know one hotel chef this way and saw what culinary needs he had that I could fill after the party was over. It turned out he needed appetizers, so I began making them on a weekly basis, and we cut a profitable deal.

Airlines

Everyone complains about airplane food. Here's your chance to do something about it. Approach international or charter carriers with ideas for providing first-class dinners every other day. They might welcome the notion of fresh meals from a local caterer. Don't forget private charters and private planes, for that matter. All pilots and passengers eat. Think of box lunches and creative picnic baskets you could provide.

Private Parties

Personal catering in private homes is always in demand and is a good source of income. Often big catering companies don't like to take on parties for fewer than thirty people. That's where you come in. A home-based, one-person caterer can handle a party of five to fifty (buffet) with just an assistant. And because you're small, you can be ready with only two days' notice.

At the start of my career, I kept private party costs down by using my clients' kitchens. I could turn out elegant and money-making dinner parties for six this way. For more than six I learned to hire a waiter. I calculated my prices with an eye on the competition and charged between $60 and $80 per person. Sometimes this gave me a profit margin of as much as 60 percent!

Local Markets and Stores

If you have a signature item—a dynamite cheesecake, dazzling cookies—think about manufacturing it. Make a few samples and take them around to local cafés and bistros. If possible, use their facility to produce at least the first few batches. That way you will be cooking in a commercial kitchen (which will help you get used to industry standards and health department regulations) while test-marketing your product. If the café owner needs persuasion, point out that he or she will reap the fruits of your labor without having to put you on the payroll.

Special Events

I started my home-based catering business by selling food to special-event planners, many in the motion-picture industry. My partner and I split the work. She did most of the food preparation while I did most of the marketing and sales.

I made up a promotional package that showed event planners the services we could provide and our wholesale catering prices. I described beautiful presentations, good working staff, superb food. Then I sent this package to public relations companies that hire caterers for press and publicity parties and anyone else connected with special events. It worked. In short order I had a potential client list of people who called me first before looking in the Yellow Pages under caterers.

In order to be legal (California law requires all caterers to manufacture their food in kitchens licensed and inspected by the California State Health Department), we prepared the food in a commercially retrofitted kitchen that we shared with a brownie manufacturer. That way two companies split one overhead. By organizing carefully my partner and I made the food for three or four big events a month. Although this sounds like a lot, we managed to do it in fifteen days, cutting expenses in half and showing a 40-percent profit.

In order to set up your business, you'll need to check the city, county, and state requirements for manufacturing food in your area. Start by calling your health department. Your local restaurant association may also have useful information. In order to protect the public's safety, many localities do not permit caterers to sell food that has been prepared in a home kitchen.

Make sure you find out the laws that pertain in your area. You'll find tips in chapter 2 on sharing and renting kitchens.

Does It Pay to Go to Cooking School?

In my experience giving parties for friends and family was easy. Nothing was too much work. No mess was too great to clean up. Even asparagus out of season wasn't too expensive for my taste. I loved it all. When it came to turning professional, however, I realized how much I didn't know about the business of entertaining. I was scared. My solution was to enroll in a professional chef's program at the California Culinary Academy in San Francisco.

Even though I had studied cooking on my own, the sixteen-month program at CCA taught me how to run a commercial kitchen and gave me good practice preparing meals for the school's 300 students. Between and after class I worked off-premise parties catered by the school and gained experience being a party manager. In class we studied with expert Chinese, Italian, and French chefs, learning techniques and presentations of classic ethnic dishes.

Best of all the school gave me a degree, recognized credentials to support me when I entered the catering field. (A list of respected culinary schools follows at the end of the book.)

Everything I did in school helped me in my career, but that doesn't mean it's the only way to go. Many of my colleagues trained by apprenticing with experienced caterers, as I did after I graduated from the CCA. Catering is learning by doing, and apprenticing gives you plenty of opportunities to do.

Apprenticeships: Learning by Doing

I worked with many different caterers after graduating from cooking school. Some were good and some were not so good, but I learned new menus and dishes from all of them. I made a practice of taking my camera along to parties in order to shoot pictures of the way the food was presented and of the decor. Afterward I had two pictures made of each shot. One I gave to my employer, who was so happy that she generally reimbursed me for the film. The other picture I kept to build my own portfolio.

Apprenticing also allowed me to make valuable contacts. As a caterer's apprentice, I met and networked with waiters, waitresses, florists, designers, and musicians whom I was able to call on when I went into business for myself.

Catering is more than cooking, I quickly learned. Catering can mean furnishing table linens, flatware, glasses, plates, even chairs for some parties. Few clients have the makings of a party for even fifteen, let alone fifty. It's up to the caterer to pull the party off, from colored tablecloths with matching napkins to comfortable chairs. Fortunately all these things are rentable, as you'll learn in chapters 8 and 9.

To find a good caterer to apprentice with, call your local rental companies and ask them about the different caterers in your area. They know which caterers are busy, organized, and successful. This information will help you decide with whom you want to work.

Learning from the Mistakes of Others

The best advice I can give you is to approach every apprenticing opportunity with an open mind. Even the worst caterer can teach you something, if only not to make his or her mistakes.

For example, early in my new career I got to a job on time and found myself alone with the staff. There we sat eating up time and money waiting for the caterer, the rentals, and the food. I couldn't help but see that being late was not only unprofitable but stressful.

Another caterer I worked with tried to befriend all her clients. She treated them like family, thinking they would forgive her slipshod style. Imagine how the father of the bride felt arriving an hour before the reception to find tables bare and the wait staff in shorts sitting around with soft drinks in their hands. I discovered on the spot how important it is to create and maintain a professional atmosphere.

At other affairs I found out what happens when a caterer runs out of food, fails to set a time for a party to end, is short a waiter, or neglects to set budget limits and stick to them. One caterer I worked for, called "Promise Them Anything" by his staff, always said yes to whatever his clients requested. When these special requests turned out to be impossible to fulfill, his staff paid the penalty. I watched an angry and disappointed client who expected one wine but received another take out his frustrations with the caterer, in front of everyone, on an innocent bartender. I made a silent vow never to put my staff in that position. (I wasn't surprised two years later to hear that "Promise Them Anything" filed for bankruptcy.)

Learning from Your Own Mistakes

Of course you can also learn a great deal from your own mistakes. Working yacht parties right after graduating from cooking school, I learned no fewer than ten lessons my first day at sea. The chef had said that he wanted a "pair of hands" to help a party on board over the Fourth of July weekend. What he didn't tell me was that the yacht was 107 feet long, with the galley situated within the last seven feet—that's all the kitchen there was. From that tiny space I was to feed eighty strangers a "make-your-own omelet" breakfast, a lunch of grilled swordfish and barbecued chicken, and two complete dinner buffets that began with appetizers.

Against all odds I succeeded, even though I forgot to
- crack and strain twenty-dozen eggs ahead of time
- slice bagels in half for easy eating
- make a backup tray of cooked bacon and sausages

- make backup bowls of butter balls and dressing
- par-boil chicken pieces before the barbecue to cut down on the cooking time
- time the appetizers and main course properly
- bring cold drinks and food for the crew
- turn the leftover swordfish into an antipasto tray
- check my equipment when I came on board
- bring a second, clean chef's jacket for dinner

Catering my first party on my own gave me a new respect for money. Cooking, I learned, was the least of my worries. The party was a financial disaster. I spent more than I collected, my waitress left with the best-looking male guest before the party was over, and I had to do the dishes alone.

Nevertheless, I survived that first party, and what I've learned since then forms the basis of this book. I'd like to spare you some of my disasters and share tips for success. I wish I had a dollar for every student who has called me after taking my catering course to tell me that all the forms I provided really worked. You'll find the same forms sprinkled throughout this book, together with information on catering courses you can take, suggested reading lists, and even tips for "culinary" computer software. Please write when the book pays off for you!

Getting Organized

Before you quit your day job and leap into catering, you need to know how much it will take to keep you afloat, which means considering some things you may never have thought about before. Sit down with pencil and paper and think about specifics. Do you have a spare room or a spare corner of a room where you can set up a home office? Do you already own an answering machine, a big mixer, and a food processor? If not, you'll need to buy them. You will also need between $3,000 and $4,000 for a business license, insurance, a lawyer, and the services of an accountant. On top of all that, remember that you will need stamps, stationery, notepads, and a calculator. You will also need to pay for your own transportation, medical insurance, and business calls.

Figure how much you need to keep going and to put money away for later. Add in something extra for emergencies and other unforeseen expenses. Ask other caterers how much of a nest egg they suggest you start with. Then make a budget by the week and the month and stick to it.

Leaving the Security of a Job

Leaving the security of a paying job is the hardest part of getting started. My solution was to begin to set up my business while I was still employed. My daily calendar read like this:

March 1: Purchase a desk and a file cabinet.
March 15: Think up a name for company.
April 2: Arrange for design of company logo.
April 17: Print cards.
May 1: Clean out spare bedroom.
May 15: Install another phone line.
June 1: Quit job.

With this system and setting aside half of each paycheck, I acquired a nest egg over several months to meet anticipated as well as unanticipated costs. I also had booked several parties by the time I left my job.

I advise the students in my seminars to try catering small parties for friends first, before they quit their day job. Turning a hobby or a passion for cooking beautiful foods into a successful career isn't going to work for everyone. You need to start small.

Of course it's no mean feat to cater a party on the weekend and still work forty hours a week, but it can be done; I know people who do it year-round. The trick is to bite off exactly what you can chew and no more. Avoid weddings for 250. Instead stick to parties of manageable size. Do a whole series of small jobs well, and before long you'll have the confidence, the

Ten Rules to Remember
to Be Successful in the Catering Business

1. Use as much creativity and take as much care with your methods of self promotion as you do with your food preparation and displays.
2. Use the services of a lawyer and an accountant.
3. Buy only from purveyors and manufacturers that sell high-quality foodstuffs and products.
4. Make sure your clients understand exactly what they are getting—through contracts and proposals—for their money.
5. Be financially smart; don't shortchange yourself or price yourself out of the market, keep impeccable records, and pay all taxes.
6. Make sure your staff clearly understands your requirements for quality, professionalism, and service.
7. Make lists—and more lists—to use before, during, and after the party.
8. Keep good records on parties, clients, employees, etc.
9. Follow-up with staff and client after the party
10. Several days after the event, review the party; learn from your mistakes and use both criticism and praise to improve future parties.

contacts, and the income stream you need to tackle more ambitious projects. At that point it will be much easier for you to figure out whether it makes sense to leave your day job.

How This Book Is Organized

Undoubtedly, you will make mistakes in your business—everyone does—but, if you read this book chapter by chapter, you'll get an excellent idea of what it takes to succeed as a home-based caterer. You'll begin by learning what you need to set up your own business, how to research the health regulations that affect caterers in your area, and how to structure your business and create a business plan. Then you'll learn how to line up work, charge for your services, find good help, and get your name around. Two full chapters discuss what it takes to stage a successful party, from planning all the way through execution. Of course keeping your books isn't nearly as fun as throwing a good party, but you'll learn that, too, along with information on the legal aspects of your catering business.

You're about to embark on an extraordinary adventure. Good luck!

2

Working Out of Your Home

During the first few days working out of your home, you may feel as though you're on vacation. No boss. No deadlines. No dress code. If it's a warm day, you may even put on shorts and take a portable phone outside in the sunshine to make sales calls. If you are to succeed, however, you'll have to become your own boss, setting working hours and daily goals. To do this effectively, it pays to take a look at your energy cycles and living patterns.

Are you a lark, bright-eyed in the morning? Or are you an owl, with energy in the afternoon? When do you feel most effective? Make sure you work hard for several hours at that time.

Don't be surprised if the demands of your new career require you to work more hours, or at least different hours, than you put in on your former job. After all, much of a caterer's work needs to be done in the evenings. Many clients can't talk about parties until after they get home from work, and if you're out delivering promotional packages and menus to prospective clients during the day, evenings may be the best time for writing proposals, going over menus, or fine-tuning events.

To give you an idea of how your day might look, consider

the following blow-by-blow description of a recent day I spent working from home:

9:00 A.M. Returned phone calls from existing clients. Made notes about changes on the party information form I had in front of me.

9:30 A.M. Called rental company to check on items needed for anniversary party on Saturday. Made sure to ask them what time they would deliver and what the total amount would be so that I could get a check from my client to give them.

10:00 A.M. Added two waiters to staff for Saturday party because guest count grew.

10:15 A.M. Started two employee folders for new waiters. Included I–9 forms and W–4's for income tax purposes. I planned to have them fill these out as soon as they arrived.

10:30 A.M. Called catering director at the hotel where I would be exhibiting bridal shower food and props on Sunday. Verified where I should park to unload.

11:00 A.M. Called fish purveyor at the specialty grocery store and got the lowest price for imported caviar for the anniversary party. Called client back with dollar quote per person. To keep costs down suggested serving caviar on blini instead of letting guests serve themselves. (*Note:* Client decided against caviar after hearing the price and stuck with the smoked salmon she chose originally.)

11:30 A.M. Called bakery to tell them that the order they filled for me last weekend had been a dozen rolls short. Deducted the price from the invoice.

11:45 A.M. Called client of last weekend's party to say what a joy it had been working there and to ask for names of three friends who might need a caterer in the future.

12:00 noon Lunched on lasagna left over from the weekend. Yum!

12:20 P.M. Tossed waiters' black aprons in the washing machine, checking pockets first. Soaked kitchen towels and chef's jacket in bleach before washing, drying, and pressing. Loaded clean jackets and towels into the van.

The Ten Most Common Mistakes That Home-Based Caterers Make

1. Not taking one day off every week

2. Setting appointments for early Monday morning after a weekend of parties

3. Answering the business phone during family time

4. Answering the family line during working hours

5. Expecting family to know and sympathize when you're worried or rushed

6. Letting friends or neighbors stay and visit when they drop in unannounced

7. Turning on the TV

8. Accepting errands from people who say, "You don't mind, do you? You're home all day!"

9. Having clients come to your home instead of meeting them at their home or office

10. Not getting up and dressed at the same time every day

12:30 P.M. Called fifteen corporate event planners from convention center referral list. Set up dates to show them my portfolio, video tapes, and suggested menu packages. Sent each one a brochure and a handwritten note telling them how much I was looking forward to our appointment.

3:30 P.M. Went to pick up film from last weekend's party and to put photographs in album for tomorrow's appointments.

4:30 P.M. Wrote out checks to suppliers for products received last weekend.

5:00 P.M. Read society page in newspaper to find upcoming events that I might attend or get involved with for business networking. Relaxed until 7 P.M.

7:00 P.M. Spent an hour on the phone calming a nervous bride. And that was an easy day!

Setting Up an Office

Working out of your home allows you to keep overhead low, but you have to create a workable environment. Although space might be at a premium in your home, it's still important to set up an area you can call your own. A quiet corner of a family room, a small room with a door, even the basement or a corner of the garage will do for a start.

To make my first work space, I divided a walk-in closet in half, placed my desk in that space, and built two shelves above my desk. From this tiny place my business grew to the point where I was booking six parties a month.

Once you've set aside office space, you'll want to outfit it with a desk, a phone on its own line, and an answering machine. A computer, a fax machine, and a copier make running everything easier, but such a cash outlay might take months to recover without a substantial client base. So wait until you really need these tools and can afford them.

For right now make sure you have the basics covered.

The first law of catering is *Make do*. Don't buy anything until you can't function without it. I've seen budding caterers run out and buy a fax machine, for example, for $400. For another $150 they install a dedicated phone line just for the fax. Then they receive all of 4 faxes a month. Sales tax and fax paper bring their investment to more than $600, so it's costing them roughly $50 a month to receive those four faxes.

If you receive fewer than twenty faxed pages a month, use a local fax machine. Some office clubs and warehouses charge as little as 5 cents per page to receive faxes and $1.00 a page to send them. The $30 or $40 you save every month will be better spent on stamps for direct-mail campaigns to introduce yourself to prospective clients or on ingredients for chocolate brownies to hand-deliver with a proposal. Sure a fax machine is convenient, but it won't impress a client or close a deal.

A computer is another matter. It stores vast amounts of information and retrieves it instantly. It saves you space and time. If you're a fast typist and can make good use of a computer,

Start-up Costs

Basic food preparation equipment	$ _____
Initial food costs and staples	$ _____
Location for cooking	$ _____
Business license	$ _____
Lawyer and accountant fees	$ _____
Insurance	$ _____
Transportation	$ _____
Advertising	$ _____
Office supplies	$ _____
Telephone	$ _____
Stationery and business cards	$ _____
Medical insurance	$ _____
Taxes	$ _____
Money to live on	$ _____
Nest egg (unexpected expenses)	$ _____
TOTAL PROJECTED START-UP COSTS	$ _____

you'll begin to think of it as your personal secretary or as an extra pair of hands.

Still, I know a caterer who grosses $1 million a year tapping out proposals on a typewriter. Information on every party she's produced is stored in old-fashioned paper files. Her best re-source is her great memory for names.

If you are catering only three or four parties a month, per-haps all you need is a filing cabinet. File parties under the date and cross-reference with the client's name. Then create an index of your party files. An up-to-date list of completed parties with the owners' names and phone numbers will be handy if quick in-formation or referrals are necessary.

You'll find that as a caterer, working within each client's budget is your biggest challenge. (There are only two kinds of clients, as the sparrow said: Cheap and cheaper.) It helps if you have first learned to work within your own budget. See how lit-tle you can spend setting up an office. Use this as an opportunity and a challenge, not as a bore and an obstacle.

For example, when I started my catering business, I decided not to buy stationery with printed letterhead. Instead I had busi-ness cards, envelopes, thank-you notes, and return-address stick-ers printed with my company logo. I never missed the letterhead. Instead I printed proposals or correspondence on a variety of different colored paper, often using clip art or photographs to jazz them up. I used cartoons, stickers, anything I could think of that was different. I wanted my proposals to stand out from the high stack of competing proposals on a client's desk.

I'm glad to say my strategy worked. Not ordering letterhead saved me $500 in the beginning. Now I don't have letterhead by choice. My proposals are lively and creative. My presentations work for me, and I'm getting interest on that $500 in the bank every day.

The moral of the story is this: In the beginning of a new ca-reer, don't get hung up on what you don't have. Concentrate in-stead on the ideas, talent, and energy you possess. Setting up an office is not that different from cooking. When a recipe calls for a spice you don't have in your cupboard, you make do. Substitu-tion and imagination are essential in running a business, too. Don't sweat the small stuff, as the saying goes. Look at the big picture.

Checklist for Your
Home Office and Supplies

Essentials

☐ Pens and pencils
☐ Ruled legal pads for taking notes
☐ File folders
☐ Filing cabinet or box
☐ Typewriter or word processor with printer for proposals
☐ Large envelopes in several sizes
☐ Stamps
☐ Return-address labels
☐ Business cards
☐ Telephone line with answering machine
☐ Calendar for marking party dates
☐ Rolodex for important names, addresses, and phone numbers
☐ Paper clips and stapler
☐ Small camera to document your work
☐ An easy-to-read clock only a glance away
☐ Start-up accounting ledger from a stationery store

What You Will Want Later

☐ Call waiting for your phone
☐ Laptop computer with catering software programs on the hard disk
☐ Personal copier
☐ An excellent bookkeeper who wants to work one or two days a week for not much money
☐ Voice mail
☐ Printed stationery, including postcards to make dropping notes to clients and purveyors easier
☐ Your own fax machine
☐ An office fridge with cold drinks and an automatic coffee/tea machine

Training Family and Friends to Take You Seriously

When you make the career transition from everyone's favorite party host to professional caterer, family and friends will need to see you in a new light. Here are some tips on training them to view you as a professional.

At first your family will think that working at home instead of going to the office means you have tons of time to run errands and tie up loose ends. Establish clear boundaries right away. Now is a good time to write down the first draft of your business plan (see chapter 3) and read it to family members. Not only will this help clarify your thoughts and get you organized, it will put your family on notice that you mean business. You will also want to explain how success in your new career will benefit everyone.

To keep family members from disturbing you while you work, make a time schedule, tack it on your office door, and stick to it. Explain to them the amount of time involved in finding clients and planning a party. Also explain why you may need to work some evenings.

Enlist your family's aid in marketing your new catering business. Perhaps your husband's corporation is planning its annual Christmas party or your daughter's basketball team is planning an awards banquet. Both events could use a caterer. There's no better representative for you than a proud relative.

Friends can also be helpful in getting your new business off the ground. Look for every chance possible to work with people you know. If a friend has a daughter getting married or a neighbor is throwing a baby shower, offer to cater the event for a nominal fee that will cover your costs. You'll get experience, and guests at the party may become future clients.

When you are first setting up shop, it is important to get your name around. Look for every opportunity to flaunt your new business. Say your son plays Little League baseball. Why not suggest a barbecue for the whole league at the local baseball field? Suddenly sixty or seventy parents know you're in business. You might even consider sponsoring a team. Not only will you have raised your profile, but by making your children part of your business, you'll have given them a sense of pride and satisfaction in what you do.

Employing Family Members

Many caterers are tempted to hire family members as employees, but before you hire them, they need to know your policies, guidelines, and rules. What do you expect from them? What can they expect from you?

For this and future hiring, you need to learn successful interviewing and hiring techniques (see chapter 4). The best way to get the results you want from an employee (family member or not) is to tell the employee exactly what he or she is expected to do, preferably in writing.

I learned this the hard way. Once I hired my sister to help me with a small party. She understood her role to mean she would go with me to the location, carry in the food, sit on a stool, critique the food, and watch me sweat as I ran around doing everything. I had pictured her passing appetizers, pouring wine, and helping with the cleanup, but I had neglected to tell her that. Later, when I exploded in the car, she simply said, "You should have told me what you wanted."

Employees who want to work for you again will often tell you what you want to hear. Family members, on the other hand, are usually more than willing to tell you when the cake is dry or the meat is overdone. Hear them out and use their feedback to improve your performance the next time.

Complying with City Ordinances

Most caterers begin working out of their homes without a business license, a caterer's permit, or product liability insurance. Because such a casual approach to running a business can get you in trouble with local and state authorities, the most important advice I can give you is to find out about government regulations in your state that pertain to catering *before* you set up shop.

Ten Common-Sense Measures
for Safe Food Handling

1. Maintain good personal hygiene and health.
2. Date and label incoming stock items and be sure everything is packaged correctly.
3. Check in and refrigerate or freeze all products the moment they arrive.
4. Rotate stock constantly.
5. Keep work areas clean, especially when you're busy.
6. Don't reuse bowls, knives, or pans without washing them first.
7. Keep pantry food on shelves and racks away from rodents and pests.
8. When in doubt, throw it out.
9. Contract for a professional extermination service.
10. Buy products from respected and approved purveyors.

Your first step should be to check with the city or county clerk's office to see whether it is legal for you to have an office in your home. Remember that regulations vary from one locality to another. In West Los Angeles it is legal for me to have my office in my home for phone and mail purposes, so long as I create no extra foot traffic.

The city business tax license issued to my home address costs about $100 a year. I got it in the city clerk's office. From there I went to the State Board of Equalization to apply for a seller's permit and resale number, which allows me to buy goods without paying taxes on them, so long as I charge sales tax to my clients. Understand that as a business, you are expected to collect the city and state tax from your clients and to turn it over quarterly to the city and state. (Check in your state; you may be lucky and not have sales tax.)

In Los Angeles I charge clients 8.25 percent of the total amount spent on food, staff, rentals, and entertainment. For more information call your own State Board of Equalization or Department of Revenue for a free tax guide.

Working as a caterer from home is trickier than working as a home-based writer or accountant because in addition to an office, you need access to a kitchen. Most state or local health protection agencies do not allow food prepared in a private home or kitchen to be sold to the public (see below). True, many caterers begin cooking out of their homes in many parts of the country, but you are risking a hefty fine if this is against the law in your area. Once you are fined, you may not be able to get a business license in the future.

Until you have established a commissary or commercial kitchen for your company (see pages 24–26), one solution is to cook in your client's home. Your client can buy the food, you can charge for your services, and you aren't breaking any laws.

Working with Your Local Health Department

As a new caterer, one of the first calls you make should be to your county health department to ask: Do I have to cook in an approved kitchen? If so, which safety and sanitation features are required for a kitchen to qualify? Generally you will find that the health department mandates such features as ventilation for the stove, stainless-steel worktables, special nonskid flooring, and thermometers in all refrigeration units.

The aim of the health department is not only to protect the public from unsafe food, but also to educate people in the food-service industry. Check with your local health department to find out what laws apply in your area. The health department staff inspects and approves kitchens on an ongoing basis. Each year, they issue me a caterer's permit, the cost of which is based on the square footage of my processing area.

Working in an approved kitchen and using your local health department as a safety resource will help ensure your success by protecting your reputation as a professional. Be sure to ask for the guidelines for bringing a kitchen up to code or building one from the ground up. Working out of an uninspected kitchen is a mistake. Not only are you breaking the law, but you run the risk of being shut down entirely.

Your local health department may also have helpful tips about ways to prevent the growth of bacteria in cooked food, transport food safely, cook and handle foods on party sites, and avoid spoilage, accidents, and illness. All this information is extremely valuable to a new caterer.

Sharing a Kitchen

Your best bet when you're first starting out is to find an approved commercial kitchen and share it with another caterer. Your goal should be to avoid the overhead of a full-time facility. To do so you will need to be resourceful and flexible, but it's worth it. Your savings in rent your first year alone can amount to $10,000 or more.

Consider running an ad in a local newspaper specifying exactly what you want. Expect a response from caterers who want to shave their overhead. A typical ad might look like this:

WANTED: Experienced Caterer to Share Commercial Kitchen

Let me help you cut your overhead. Share 8 to 15 days a month. My flexible schedule of clients can accommodate your business.

Own many props and decor pieces to share. City licensed and insured. Extensive knowledge in safety and sanitation.

Excellent references from industry professionals.

In deciding which kitchen to share, you'll want to consider how near it is to your home and how much parking there is for pickups and deliveries. Also look at the layout, size, equipment, and storage areas. It's not likely you'll want to spend thousands of dollars to outfit a rental kitchen, so finding one that best suits your needs is the goal.

A well-designed kitchen will save you time, money, and product. First look for stairs and steps. Everything on one level is most desirable. Are there double doors for big floral arrangements or props? Are there screen doors with overhead fly-traps? Is the floor in smooth condition? Are there thick, black rubber mats to protect your legs when standing? Are the walls free of holes? Is there enough room for your entire crew to work side by side in the busiest months? Are there adequate bathroom facilities for your employees, if you hire any, with extra hand sinks? Are there tables and chairs for workers to sit and eat at? Is the equipment in reasonably good shape? Have the ovens been calibrated recently and the refrigeration temperatures checked with thermometers? Is the place freshly painted? Are storage areas accessible and dry?

If a kitchen has been recently approved by your local health department, building and safety department, and fire department, you should be issued your own necessary caterer's permit without any problem.

Make sure you're not violating any existing lease and zoning laws. A real estate broker or an attorney will suggest the right questions to ask and help you work out the best agreement with your co-tenant or landlord.

My first catering partner and I shared commercial kitchen space in Santa Monica with a brownie manufacturer who sold other caterers great dessert trays. The only major piece of equipment we had to buy when moving in was a double-door reach-in refrigerator. Stoves, worktables, shelves, and a freezer were there and included in our lease. We didn't need a walk-in refrigerator; instead, we rented refrigerator trucks at weekend rates when we needed to transport a lot of food for large parties.

Your goal should be to share space that includes just about everything you need in the way of heavy equipment. If you find yourself in a position where you need to invest in refrigeration equipment, it pays to buy the best you can. Poor refrigeration shortens the life of your product, reduces the quality, and adds to your food cost by increasing spoilage. Commercial refrigerators such as Traulsen or Hobart are designed to keep food at lower temperatures than average home refrigerators can maintain.

Dishwashers are sometimes missing from commercial kitchens, but you can lease them from food brokers or restaurant supply houses. I negotiated a good deal for a brand-new dishwasher with a cleaning supply company by signing a two-year detergent contract and rodent-control program.

Renting a Kitchen on a Per-Day Basis

If you only need a kitchen two or three days a month, look into day rentals from private clubs or churches. Often places like these use their kitchens only a couple of days a week, and the rest of the time they stand empty. Without signing a lease you can negotiate a per-day price and use the kitchen only when you need to. Most of the time these types of kitchens have been commercially retrofitted and approved by the health department, but you'll have to check.

Outfitting Your Kitchen

Let's assume that you've decided on a kitchen. Your next challenge is to figure out what you need in the way of pots, pans, and other equipment to do a good job. Unless you've worked for some time in a professional kitchen, you probably don't know much about commercial-quality equipment. The best way to learn is to visit a restaurant-supply house with the checklist on page 28 in hand.

You'll notice immediately that pots, pans, food processors, and the rest of the equipment you see is larger and heavier than the equipment you use in your home kitchen. It has to be sturdier in order to hold large quantities of food and to stand up to constant use. Everything costs more than the home kitchen version, too. You can expect to pay anywhere from $3,000 to $5,000 if you're starting from scratch.

If you don't already own them, you will need assorted sizes

of sauté pans and saucepans, sheet pans, chafing-dish liners, and roasting pans to prepare, deliver, and serve food. Be sure to get sizes that fit both home and commercial ovens, as you'll be cooking in your clients' home kitchens as well as in your own commercial setup.

Stainless-steel mixing bowls, colanders, and strainers are important and come in all prices. Find the most durable.

Also get a lot of clear plastic storage containers with lids in every size. You'll need a couple of insulated box carriers for transporting food to and from party sites. And don't forget to invest in a few rolls of heavy-duty plastic wrap and aluminum foil.

Get special equipment, as you need it, for offbeat recipes (madelines, for example) or new party menus. A good source of such equipment is industry trade shows such as the Fancy Food Show or The National Restaurant Association Show at the McCormick Center in Chicago. Equipment purveyors haunt those places. You can buy anything from pots and pans to walk-in refrigerators, but you can also find such novelties as chocolate mints to imprint with your company logo or lace wrappers for your halved lemon garnishes. For example, I once found thermal holding bags for bakers' racks at the Western Foodservice Show in San Francisco at the Moscone Center. I still use these nifty bags—which cost me $200—to keep my warm desserts at the right temperature and to protect them at party sites.

Smallwares and Utensils

As a caterer you'll be dealing with a jumble of small items: metal and wooden spoons, whisks, spatulas, tongs of different lengths, funnels, vegetable peelers, matches, pastry brushes, cake-decorating tips and bags.

The first thing you need is a storage place so that you'll be able to find each item when you need it. A metal or plastic toolbox works fine. So does a fishing-tackle box. Look for them at a hardware or building-supply store. Any of these boxes is a natural for organizing kitchen tools.

Kitchen Supplies Checklist

Pots and Pans in All Different Sizes

- [ ] sauté pans
- [ ] roasting pans
- [ ] stockpots
- [ ] saucepans with covers
- [ ] sheet pans, full and half size
- [ ] chafer liners
- [ ] stainless mixing bowls

Utensils

- [ ] small and large ladles
- [ ] tongs of differnt lengths
- [ ] kitchen spoons
- [ ] measuring spoons
- [ ] measuring cups
- [ ] carving board
- [ ] cutting boards
- [ ] spatulas
- [ ] wire whisks
- [ ] potato peelers
- [ ] can opener
- [ ] colanders
- [ ] knifes of different sizes
- [ ] wooden spoons

- [ ] portion scale
- [ ] scissors
- [ ] strainers
- [ ] pepper grinder
- [ ] pot holders
- [ ] towels
- [ ] corkscrew

Appliances

- [ ] freestanding mixer with two bowls
- [ ] food processor
- [ ] blender
- [ ] ice-cream maker
- [ ] coffeepot (for crew)
- [ ] portable slicer

Housekeeping

- [ ] garbage cans
- [ ] broom and dustpan
- [ ] mops
- [ ] buckets
- [ ] first-aid kit
- [ ] carpet sweeper
- [ ] cleaning supplies

What to Look for in a Good Knife

Since a knife is a chef's most important piece of equipment, you'll want to look for good knives that will last a lifetime and a long, thin steel whetstone to keep the blades sharp. You want a sharp short-bladed knife not only because it makes cutting easier, but also because a dull blade can give you a nasty cut more quickly than a sharp one can.

When you go shopping for a knife, notice the variety of blades and handles. Heft a few knives before you buy to see which ones feel best in your hand. Most blades today are made from high-carbon stainless steel, which has the strength of stainless steel plus carbon steel's ability to hold an edge. Not only is it stronger than stainless steel, it does not discolor on contact with high-acid foods, such as tomatoes or onions, or rust if not dried immediately. Though some knife handles are still made of wood, these eventually crack and split. Most handles today are plastic, made to look and feel like wood, and they have the same life span as the knife blade.

Trident-Wurstef or Henckel are two brands that I can recommend. No matter what knives you buy, use your steel to sharpen them every time you use them and have all knives professionally sharpened once a year.

When I set up shop, I bought a starter set of Henckels from a catalog. It included a chef's knife, a boning knife, a slicer, and a couple of paring knives. That was all I needed for several years. These sets, easily available to home chefs, are a bargain for the new professional.

Setting Up Your Pantry

Every caterer needs to set up a pantry in order to be ready for last-minute parties. As you bring in dry goods, you'll need to calculate what I call your "*mise en place*" cost. This is French for "everything in its place." That means flour, salt, spices, and other staples stocked and ready to be used before you buy the perishables for your first event.

If you keep careful track of your receipts, you can incorporate these costs into your per-person food charge. I calculate a per-person party "*mise en place*" figure by dividing the monthly cost of staples by the number of people I plan to serve that month.

Staples Checklist

Dry Goods
- [ ] matches
- [ ] doilies
- [ ] votive candles
- [ ] toothpicks
- [ ] cocktail napkins
- [ ] Sterno
- [ ] garbage-can liners
- [ ] foil and film wrap
- [ ] take-out containers
- [ ] aluminum pans
- [ ] parchment paper

Coffee Supplies
- [ ] coffee, regular and decaffeinated
- [ ] nondairy cream and sugar packets

- [ ] artificial sweetener
- [ ] herbal and regular tea
- [ ] drink stirrers

Refrigerator Condiments
- [ ] butter
- [ ] mayonnaise
- [ ] mustard
- [ ] cream cheese
- [ ] catsup
- [ ] lemon and lime juice

Dry Ingredients
- [ ] spice-rack assortment
- [ ] salt and pepper
- [ ] flour
- [ ] sugar
- [ ] crackers

Transportation

After a job or two you'll find that carrying the food, props, equipment, and staff is an important part of catering. A van, a jeep, or a truck is the best thing for a caterer to work from, although loading and unloading are always a challenge. Think about conserving your energy so that you don't get hurt. Practice careful lifting. A dolly or a hand truck is essential for getting everything on and off easily.

If you don't already own a van, don't rush out and buy one. By doing your homework and charting the number of days you're likely to need a van each month, you will see why it makes better sense for your cash flow to rent for eight days a month than to own for thirty. My strategy is to rent vans and trucks as I need them. I built a good relationship with a van rental company in my community. I asked for and got bargain weekend rates and weekly rates when I needed them. I even managed a monthly rate for December (the biggest party month) by reserving early. You can do the same. Remember to pass the cost of renting a van on to your client when you figure your costs per head (see chapter 8).

Establishing Relationships with Wholesale Purveyors

Until now you've probably purchased all of your meats, fish, produce, and other supplies at a grocery store. When you go into business for yourself, however, you can no longer afford to buy food at retail prices. Buying wholesale will save you 10 to 35 percent, and you'll enjoy a better selection to boot. Research wholesale purveyors in your area; find out how long each company you're considering has been in business, whether they're licensed and insured like you, and whether the two of you see eye to eye on supplying the finest product to your clients. One of the best ways to find out about quality purveyors is to ask other caterers.

A good working relationship with a purveyor's sales representative can save you time designing your menus, can help you control your food cost, and can even help you solve food production problems. Sales reps are knowledgeable about how to calculate the right portions, how to keep food from spoiling, and how to take advantage of the availability of special seasonal items.

I work primarily with three different wholesale food purveyors. I'm able to buy chicken and fish from one, dry goods and beef from another, and produce, flowers, and fresh pasta from the third. I do almost all my shopping over the phone, which saves me considerable amount of time, gas, and money. I've used these same purveyors for the past ten years. Not only do they sell the finest quality foods but they also take the time to negotiate price, suggest alternative products, and provide safe packaging and reliable delivery (even to the party site if I've forgotten anything). After years of a successful business relationship, I've also reaped the benefits of building a solid credit history and have thirty days to pay my invoices if I need it.

My network of purveyors has supplied me with tips on finding good staff, with job leads, and even with presentation ideas. As we often say in the trade, you're only as good as your purveyors. Make sure you find the best.

Your Next Step

By the time you've read this chapter carefully, you'll have learned how to set up a home office, how to enlist the help of family and friends, and how much equipment to buy (and where) to get started. You're a lot closer to catering your first party than you were thirty pages ago. But before you jump in, take the time to create a formal business plan, the subject of the next chapter.

3
Writing a Business Plan
or How to Avoid Financial Disaster

Running a successful business is like cooking a meal: The more time and care you put into the preparation, the better the results. In this chapter you will learn how to write a business plan. In the process you will learn how to take yourself and your business seriously.

If you have not run a business before, consider attending seminars on starting and running a business. Check local colleges or business schools for courses taught by financial experts. Such courses are invaluable, and the fees are usually reasonable.

Local business organizations can also be helpful, both in increasing your visibility and in gaining you access to good advice. When I first started out, I joined a local chamber of commerce group that invited consultants and professionals to speak at weekly breakfast meetings. An added bonus of my membership was the chance to network and share information with other business people, including other caterers. To get started yourself, pick up the phone and call a local chapter of Rotary, Kiwanis, or another business group. Ask if you might attend as a guest the first few times.

In your search for free information on running a business, be sure not to overlook your local library. Look for texts or videos on business problems and management. Also ask the manager of your favorite bookstore for any outstanding books written by or about new entrepreneurs.

Not far from my house, I discovered that the local chapter of the California Restaurant Association had a library available for members' use. No one was ever there. I had the place and all its books to myself. I read all about marketing a food business and writing profitable menus.

Certain government services may also be worth investigating. For example, I learned from a flier I found in the city clerk's office that the Small Business Administration makes retired business people available as consultants to budding entrepreneurs. My partner and I spent hours with an accountant who had owned and managed his own firm for thirty-five years. He helped us project and estimate our first-year financial data, pointing out start-up costs, showing us how to keep an accounting ledger, and teaching us about gross profit margin and standard operating percentages. Working as a consultant not only filled his needs (he missed his business) but also helped us as partners to understand the necessity of good accounting practices from day one. Call your local Small Business Administration office and ask about SCORE (Service Corps of Retired Executives). Also check the SBA Hotline Desk at (800) 827–5722 and ask for *The Small Business Directory,* a free guide that tells you what videos and books are available for purchase.

How to Structure Your Business

Before you can write a business plan, you need to know what sort of business you plan to operate. Will you operate as a sole proprietor? Or do you plan to have one or more partners? Does it make sense for you to incorporate? These are some of the questions we'll explore. Before you make any decision, however, be sure to consult a certified public accountant.

The structure of your business depends on your background, skills, and interests. Often caterers start as sole proprietors and later expand into partnerships. The appeal of operating as a sole proprietor is that it's easy. You're in control, you don't have many start-up costs, and the record keeping required by law is minimal. Any money you make is simply taxed as personal income. The disadvantage is that you personally are liable for any business debts you incur for the rest of your life.

A partnership is also low in start-up costs. Like the sole proprietorship (and unlike a corporation), it's relatively free of government control. Profit from the partnership to the partners is taxed as personal income, and the partnership is required to file an information return. One real advantage is that with a compatible partner working at your side from the start, your new business has a broader base of knowledge and two people to share the problems.

The trick is to make the terms of your partnership agreement as explicit as possible. My catering partner and I began by dividing our responsibilities according to our interests and talents. We decided that she would take care of the food ordering, purchases, and cooking and I would meet with clients and deal with sales and marketing. We had our attorney draw up an agreement to reflect our understanding of our roles and to minimize problems and surprises later. The agreement listed what personal equipment was brought to the partnership, the hours each of us was expected to work, the days we had off, what time of year we could vacation, how we intended to divide the profit each month, what percentage of profit we would put back into the company each year, and even what to do in the event of one partner's death. (We each purchased our own insurance policy and made the other partner the beneficiary upon death. In this way we created cash—the insurance money—for the remaining partner to purchase the deceased partner's interest based on a preset value.)

We took plenty of time to talk it over so that we both knew what the other person expected. If you are interested in establishing a formal partnership, you might take a look at *The Partnership Book: How to Write a Partnership Agreement* by Denis Clifford and Ralph Warner, published by Nolo Press.

The disadvantages of a partnership are similar to the disadvantages of a sole proprietorship, but they're multiplied by the number of partners. The main disadvantage is that each partner has unlimited liability for the partnership's debts. If your partner orders up $10,000 in new equipment and then skips town, you're stuck with the bill.

Also, remember that a partnership means divided authority. As a sole proprietor, you don't have to compromise; as a partner you can't avoid it. For this reason getting along with and trusting your partner are absolutely critical. In fact finding a suitable one might be the hardest thing you ever do, short of finding a suitable mate.

Your third option for structuring your company is to set it up as a corporation. The appeal of a corporation is that it may allow you to limit your personal liability in the event the corporation incurs debts you can't repay. It's also much easier to raise investment capital if you incorporate and to make sure that the business will continue if you die.

Each state has different corporate record-keeping requirements. A good accountant should be able to acquaint you with what's involved before you take the plunge. You'll also want your business to be making enough money to benefit from the corporate structure; otherwise you may be stuck paying a hefty minimum tax, whether you can afford it or not.

If you decide to incorporate, you will need the advice of an attorney in setting up. The initial costs and filing fees vary, depending on the attorney's fees and state regulations. Remember that as a corporate entity, you're subject to double taxation—first on the corporation's profits and later on the salary you pay yourself.

Writing a Business Plan

Now that you've decided how you want to structure your business, you're ready to write your business plan. This meaty document is intended to help you express your plans, both immediate and long term, as concretely as possible. If you're hoping to get a bank loan or to raise money from outside investors, you can't

The Ten Most Common Mistakes That New Businesspeople Make

1. Failing to ask for professional assistance when you need it
2. Waffling when it comes to making decisions
3. Failing to remedy a lack of confidence
4. Making bad budgets
5. Borrowing too much money or using too much credit
6. Extending too much credit
7. Not anticipating market trends
8. Keeping inadequate financial records
9. Failing to project a favorable public image
10. Underpricing your service or products

do without a business plan. Even if you plan to work alone and pay as you go, writing a detailed business plan is an informative and challenging exercise.

A business plan isn't something you whip together in a few days. In fact I usually give my catering students an entire semester to pull it together. None of them wants to do it, of course. I hear all sorts of groans and mumbling about "not having time." My reply is: "You can't afford not to make the time." Starting a business without a plan is like getting in a car to go on a long trip without a map or any gas. You simply won't get where you think you're going.

Writing a business plan is the best way I know to create a vision of your company. It's a tool you can use to measure and then improve your performance. It offers a basis for making decisions, defines your partnership if you have one, and ultimately lets you share your vision with employees. Of course some sections described below—particularly company management and projections for the future—may be tough to write when you're just starting out. My advice is to put these sections aside until you have enough information and experience to go on.

The Eight Parts of a Typical Business Plan

1. Summary Statement: An Overview of Your Business
2. Market Analysis: Defining Your Niche
3. Organizational Chart and Staffing
4. Management Plan
5. Marketing Strategy
6. Menus
7. Financial Data
8. Projections: The Future of Your Business

Step One:
Writing the Summary Statement

Starting with your business name and location, write an overview of your business. Tell who you are, your credentials for starting your business, the market you plan to reach, and your plans for dealing with the competition. Then give a good, clear idea of your goals and objectives, including your plans for the future.

Some business consultants suggest writing the summary statement last; once you've got the entire plan on paper, it's a cinch to summarize. I prefer writing the summary statement first because I need to focus my energy and inspiration on the project. Either way works.

The first few paragraphs of a summary statement for a new home-based catering company might look like this:

> Food Fanatics caters parties for private individuals and businesses in Los Angeles County. Started by Denise Vivaldo, the company specializes in parties where the decor is just as spectacular as the food. Many of the company's clients come from the city's entertainment industry. Clients call not only when they want value for their money but especially when they want to create a memorable and complete environment for their guests.
>
> Food Fanatics' mission statement is printed on its business

cards: The company strives to produce first-class menus for any occasion and to complement the vision of its clients. Everyone with whom Food Fanatics works—from waiters, bartenders, and hostesses to rental companies, florists, and entertainers—must meet its high standards.

What distinguishes Food Fanatics from other caterers in the area is Ms. Vivaldo's extensive background in food and wine. Having cooked in Shanghai, Cairo, San Francisco, Tokyo, New Orleans, Rome, and Honolulu, she is an expert in an unusually broad range of food styles.

Step Two:
Defining Your Niche

This section gives you the opportunity to understand your market, size up the competition, and define your specialty.

Begin by developing a list of competitors. Consult the Yellow Pages under "caterers." Be sure to check restaurant listings, too. Highlight ads that mention take-out food, banquets, or special events. Then pick up the phone and talk to the owners and managers of these places. Ask them what dollar volume they did last year and how many years they've been in business. Most owners or operators are happy to share information because they're either winning or losing the game. While you're on the phone, you should also try to find out the biggest problem they face from year to year and how they solve it. Obviously once you have talked to everybody in town, you'll have a much better idea of the sort of competition you're up against.

Another option is to hire professionals for a demographic study. Often restaurant management firms have up-to-date information on hotel chains or restaurants currently in "plan check" (that is, waiting for approval from the city building and safety department). Most likely their information is not free, but you can negotiate—maybe you can provide them with a fabulous Christmas party.

If you're planning to market a product or service to restaurants or other caterers, it's even easier for you to do market research. One caterer I worked with recently wanted to introduce a premium chocolate-covered fortune cookie. She didn't know whether people would like it or not. I told her to call every caterer in town to see who was interested in buying it. Armed with their positive response, she went ahead.

When you're ready to write up this section of your business plan, focus on the opportunities and challenges that lay ahead for your new business. What are you offering that other caterers don't offer? What audience are you targeting? What are the demographics for your area? How's the local economy? Can you define the niche that you'd like to fill? How do you know that your service is a valuable addition to the community?

A typical market analysis might look like this:

Orange Blossom Catering
Redondo Beach, California

Redondo Beach is a very desirable place to live and offers a wonderful climate on a year-round basis to its 65,000 residents. In addition, within a three-mile radius there are 175,000 residents and within a five-mile radius 366,000 people.

The most prominent age group is from twenty to forty-four, prime ages for first and second marriages and other special events. The average income within a three-mile radius is $53,000 per household.

Nation's Business magazine predicts that today's altar-bound couples can afford and want the works. In 1990 more than 2.4 million couples were married, and of that number 64 percent were first marriages. *Bride* magazine estimates that first-time couples spent $28 billion on weddings this year, and of that amount $5.9 billion went to receptions.

Southern California leads the nation in the bridal market; $2.7 billion is spent annually in bridal-related products and services. Unlike other regional areas California's bridal market is year-round.

Given the lack of upscale, full-service catering companies in this area, Orange Blossom Catering expects the community to give its full support as clients. With the current strength of the bridal market, it is an excellent time for Orange Blossom Catering to enter this special-event market.

Step Three:
Drawing Your Organizational Chart

A typical organizational chart for a catering business run from your home might look like this:

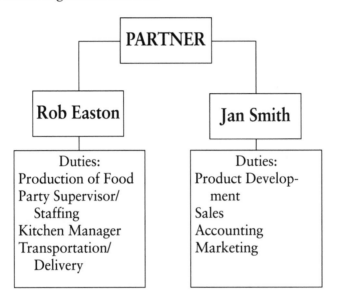

The number of employees you have at any given moment will vary depending on the size of the parties you cater. (For much more about employees, see chapter 4.)

It makes good sense to include in this section a copy of a staff sheet from a recent event showing how many chefs and waiters it took to do the job. Indicate what each employee did and how much they got paid, as shown on pages 42–43.

If you're writing your business plan for the purposes of getting a loan or raising money, you'll want to write a paragraph on where you get your staff, the techniques you use to train them, and your experience in handling employees.

Sweet Treats Catering Staff Sheet

Party Date _____   Party Coordinator _____

Party File Number _____   Party Name _____

Employee Name	Job Description	Time in/out	Rate per hour

Date				
9/11	Alan Dune	Party Manager	4 pm/11 pm	$15/hour

Responsibilities: Buffet decor, dinner timing and serving with kitchen, staff check-in, waiter job assignments, staff breaks, feeding musicians, locking up gifts, party breakdown, separating linens, washing, storing, and securing all rentals until pickup.

9/11	Cheryl Flower	Chef	2 pm/9 pm	$12/hour

Responsibilities: Leave kitchen with food and loaded van; drive to location; set up temporary work kitchen; heat, finish, and serve appetizers, dinner buffet; and help bakery set up wedding cake. Direct job assignments to kitchen assistant. Refill buffet as needed, oversee breakdown of kitchen, leave kitchen clean, remove all garbage, recycle cans and bottles, repack van, and off-load at commissary. Put any extra food in the commissary refrigerator.

9/11	Fred Stone	Server	5 pm/10 pm	$10/hour

Responsibilities: Buffet monitor: Count plates; roll silverware; polish glasses; fill and light chafers; check tables for ashtrays, salt and pepper, and water pitchers. Pass appetizers as guests arrive, help serve buffet, bus dirty dishes and glasses. Arrange furniture back in living room at end of party.

9/11	Steve Higgenson	Kitchen Assistant	3 pm/9 pm	$ 8/hour

Responsibilities: Meet Chef Cheryl at location and help unload van. Start grill. Grill swordfish steaks halfway, finish in rental oven, sauté green beans for chafers, carve beef tenderloin on the buffet, help clean up and break down buffet and temporary kitchen. Drive to commissary and help Cheryl unload van after party.

Such a paragraph might look like this:

I plan to use culinary students, local college students, and/or servers who have impressed me with their skill and training. I will provide each server with a job description and list of policies. Everyone will also receive a party flow sheet to round out the details of the event. Finally, before the event, we will meet to discuss the overall game plan and answer any questions. My experience working in restaurants and with other caterers has made me a firm believer in hiring polite and considerate people who can think on their feet.

Step Four:
Describing Company Management and Operation

This section has four parts:

1. *Key personnel* Bios of your company's key players go first. Be sure to emphasize special talents and attach up-to-date résumés. How you "sell" your management skills to an interested investor, partner, or loan officer may mean the difference between success and failure.

2. *Office and kitchen plans* Next include a description of your office setup and your plan for either sharing, renting, building, or buying an approved kitchen. The results of your research into permits, licenses, and health regulations belong here. Indicate that you intend to conform to any legal requirements that affect you. You want any loan officer reading your business plan to know that you intend to be a full-time, legal caterer, not just a weekend warrior.

3. *Capital investments* If you have made capital investments in office furniture or kitchen equipment, list them here. Note the priority and importance of your purchases. If items have already paid for themselves, say so.

4. *First year's operating agenda* This is where you lay out a specific operating plan. A three-month schedule of events for a small home-based caterer might look like this:

January
- Place ad in local paper inviting "This Year's Spring Brides" to call my wedding consultant hot line. Answer one question, get their name and number and send them a letter of introduction explaining the complimentary services I provide as their caterer.
- Attend local bridal fair and leave each vendor with a wrapped "Mexican wedding cake cookie," together with a price list by the dozen. "This is something I'm selling as the first edible party favor for every bride to order."

February
- Contact American Heart Association regarding its annual bake sale.
- Send valentine cookies to PTA board.
- Call local food editor, pitch article on the "Spring Bounty of Vegetables."

March
- Deliver six "American-Made Lunch Boxes" to the local convention-center meeting planners. Follow up from my "cold calls" of last December about supplying lunch boxes and brownie baskets. Leave a typed price list with each lunch box.
- Give complete written proposal to the convention center's director of operations about the convention center purchasing one hundred boxes and baskets for its annual employee party and gift giveaways.
- Check with local ad agencies for campaigns featuring "real business people" as the models. Find out to whom to address a promo pack with pictures. Stress that I would be happy to appear in the ad and feed the crew.

Step Five:
Your Marketing Plan

Creating an image for your company, attracting new customers, and establishing referral business are the essence of marketing.

In this section of your business plan, you need to commit to paper all your strategies for increasing your exposure within the community and for drumming up business.

Advertising and promotional ideas Provide time and cost estimates for the twelve-month operating agenda you provided in step four. (See chapter 6 for additional ideas.)

A useful exercise (and a necessary one if you're creating a business plan as a formal document designed to appeal to loan officers or investors) is to include a sample ad for the Yellow Pages. If you plan on running any other ads, illustrate them in this section and specify the schedule and costs involved as well. Also consider whether direct mail is for you. A simple postcard with a recipe can work wonders; detail how many cards you plan to send out, at what cost, and include a sample.

If you have a celebrity client or well-known relative, seek out a way you can utilize their visibility to help market your business. Include letters of recommendation in your business plan or thank-you letters you've received on clients' letterhead.

This section should also describe the networking you plan to do in your community and any other ways you hope to garner new business.

Long-term strategy Keeping your business going over the long haul is the name of the game. To do that you need to consider the marketing steps you'll be taking two or three years from now to keep customers calling.

Chapter 6 discusses long-term strategies. Once you've chosen those that appeal to you, describe them and the costs involved in this section.

Pricing and services What services you intend to offer and how you intend to charge for them are both part of your marketing plan. Stress the service or services you will be able to provide for your clients that are different from anybody else's in the marketplace today. Perhaps you cook without salt and use only fresh herbs from a local organic garden. Say as much. After all, offering products like everyone else's won't help you stand out.

Most new businesses fail in the first year from underpricing their products. As you consider what to charge for your product and services, remember that.

Step Six:
Creating a Menu

A menu is the strongest marketing tool you have, yet most caterers never print one up. Making up menus as you go along to suit clients' desires has become the norm. Such an approach is certainly creative, but it's also costly. Perfecting a number of dishes can save you time, money, and mistakes. Plan from the start to design menus for profit and success and include menus in your business plan. Make sure that you describe each dish well enough so that people will be hungry simply reading about them. (See chapter 6 for more information on designing winning menus.)

This is the section of your business plan where you'll also want to describe your plans for making and marketing a signature item. For example, my partner made the best lemon ginger cake in Los Angeles. The more I sold, the more clients wanted. Describe your plans for your signature item and indicate your profit margin.

If your business plan is intended to open doors for you, let your reader know that you intend to review your menus, food-cost percentages, and profit margins every six months.

Step Seven:
Crunching the Numbers

This section, filled to the brim with financial data, is where you discuss the nuts and bolts of your business. Being realistic about "the numbers" is your only chance of survival and long-term success.

With personal computers, accounting programs, and some good advice from a friendly accountant, financial statements are easy to create and understand. After all, financial statements are nothing more than simple arithmetic. Don't let unfamiliar terminology scare you off. It's harder to make perfect soufflés for one hundred guests than it is to balance a budget.

A standard business plan includes the following:

Balance sheets   Compile a list of your assets and liabilities. Assets include all cash, party deposits, accounts receivable (contracted future money), and an inventory of the value of everything physical that makes up your company—food products, equipment, even the leasehold on your kitchen. Liabilities include accounts payable (the amounts you owe to purveyors) and any other debts you have to pay each month.

Total up each column, subtract liabilities from assets, and you have your equity, or your company's net worth.

Income statements (also called profit and loss statements or P&Ls)   You'll need to create two different P&Ls for your business plan. The first one is a monthly analysis of income and expenses. Using an actual month's sales and expenses, figure out the day-to-day cost of running your business.

Your second P&L should project your income and expenses over the next twelve months. Take into account as many variables that might affect sales as you can: national holidays, taxes, harsh weather, religious days. An example: November is notoriously bad for caterers. People stay home for Thanksgiving and cook their own turkey. Everyone is getting ready for Christmas and saving their entertaining dollars for December. And November's weather can't be trusted, so brides steer clear. (If you need some data on industry trends or national figures to help with your projections, contact The National Association of Catering Executives for valuable statistics. Call (502) 583–3783 or write 314 West Liberty, Suite 201, Louisville, KY 40202.

Cash flow statements   Here you compare the amount of cash coming in with the amount of cash going out. Make out twelve statements, one for each month. Be sure to include bills you pay only on a quarterly basis.

As you project your cash flow, remember that deciding on what terms you'll bill your clients is essential to cash flow. It is

Monthly Statement

INCOME

Gross Sales	$32,833
Cost of Labor	5,875
Cost of Food & Beverage	7,875
Cost of Transportation	650
Total of three = Cost of sales	14,400
Gross Profit	**$18,433**

OPERATING EXPENSES

Rent	$1,500
Utilities/Phone	550
Owner's salary	2,600
Payroll/Benefits/Taxes	3,350
Advertising/Promotion	900
Accounting/Legal	900
Office supplies	300
Linen service	200
Insurance	630
License/Taxes	250
Depreciation	250
Interest	195
Equipment maintenance	230
Miscellaneous	400
Total Expenses	**$12,255**

NET PROFIT BEFORE TAXES	**$6,178**
NET PROFIT AS A PERCENTAGE OF GROSS SALES	**18.8%**

Sample Cash Flow Statement

	January	February	March	1st Quarter
Expenses				
Food	_____	_____	_____	_____
Staff	_____	_____	_____	_____
Insurance	_____	_____	_____	_____
Rentals	_____	_____	_____	_____
Other expenses	_____	_____	_____	_____
	_____	_____	_____	_____
	_____	_____	_____	_____
TOTALS:	_____	_____	_____	_____
Income				
Deposit	_____	_____	_____	_____
Balance	_____	_____	_____	_____
Other Income	_____	_____	_____	_____
	_____	_____	_____	_____
TOTALS:	_____	_____	_____	_____

standard business practice to collect a deposit for at least half of the event bill when you sign the contract. As a convenience to my clients, I get the balance in full five days before their party. Then with the excitement of the day, they don't have to do bookkeeping. Of course the initial deposit must be enough to cover all your out-of-pocket costs.

Step Eight: Projections for the Future

There's a saying in catering that you're only as good as your last party. Referrals based on your good reputation are the mainstays of continuing success. You listed your strategy for insuring repeat and referral business as part of step five. In this section project how those plans will translate into dollars. Be sure to chart how much growth you expect in the next few years and also what you anticipate in the way of challenges.

I closed my own business plan this way:

Living in the country's trendiest city keeps me on my toes about changes in America's life-style. I know keeping current on the public's eating habits is a full-time job. And in the last ten years I've been able to predict needs and supply what my clients have asked for.

As the national economy changed and the decadent eighties came to a close, I didn't need a crystal ball to know that the nineties would be a decade during which I would be selling and producing greater value for the client's dollar.

I've told my clients for years that it's easy to build a beautiful buffet with lots of money, but it takes talent to make a fabulous presentation with no dollars and a ball of string. What I offer every client is my desire to anticipate challenges and enjoy the opportunity to meet them head on. I never say it's going to be easy, but creating memorable, exciting, and profitable parties is plain, old, wonderful fun.

My favorite referral and compliment came from former Senator John Tunney. "Denise is a phantom, she moves fast, her staff is beyond trained, and the fund-raiser went so smoothly, I'm still not sure she was there!"

Business Books, Software, and Videos

Books

Getting Organized by Stephanie Winston, Warner Books, 1978
The Organized Executive by Stephanie Winston, Warner Books, 1985

If You Haven't Got Time to Do It Right, When Will You Find the Time to Do It Over? by Jeffrey Mayer, Simon & Schuster, 1991

The Seven Habits of Highly Effective People by Stephen R. Covey, Simon & Schuster, 1989

Talk Your Way to Success by Lilyan Wilder, Eastside Publishing, 1991

Software
"Plan Write " by Business Resource Software
2013 Wells Branch Parkway
Austin, Texas 78728
(800) 423–1228

"Biz Plan Builder" By Jian
127 Second Street
Los Altos, CA 94022
(800) 346–5426

Videos
Small Business Video Library
P.O. Box 908
Arlington, VA 22216
(800) 225–2468

Volume I, Marketing: Winning Customers with a "Workable" Plan

Volume II, The Business Plan: Your Roadmap for Success

Volume III, Promotion: Solving the Puzzle

Volume IV, Home-Based Business: A Winning Blueprint

4

Knowing the Legal Aspects
of Your Catering Business

Although every new business owner makes mistakes, there are certain areas where you really don't want to make a misstep. In this chapter we'll discuss when to call an attorney, why you have to have insurance, how you can protect yourself and your clients with contracts, as well as the costs, responsibilities, and obligations you have to your employees. In addition we'll cover employee management techniques, good rules for good employee/ employer relations, and how to document each relationship in your business.

Why You Need a Good Attorney

As we've already seen, an attorney can be helpful in setting up your company or helping you write a partnership agreement. An attorney can also help you negotiate and understand your lease when you rent or share a kitchen and help you verify ordinances governing the use of the property. In older leaseholds local ordinances have often been ignored, and new tenants find themselves in violation of zoning laws and thus unable to conduct business legally. You want to know your rights as a tenant and your landlord's legal obligations to you. The safety of your company and any employees you may have depend on it.

Though it may seem expensive to talk to an attorney, I think of it as preventive medicine. I don't want my business to get sick from laws I don't know about.

As our catering business grew, my partner and I worked with our attorney regularly. As our parties became more complex and expensive, the one-page agreement we first used grew into a several-page contract that protected our clients and us from events beyond our control.

An attorney taught me to discuss with clients any potential problems that might arise during the planning of an event. He taught me to make notes and document what I promised in the weeks of preparty planning. Both these measures helped avoid unpleasant surprises.

Staying informed of current legislation about employer/ employee relations is also your attorney's job. Whether you have one employee or twenty, you'll need to update your information constantly. Just ask your attorney about new legislation as well as worker's compensation and unemployment insurance.

Insurance:
Can't Live with the Premiums,
Can't Live with the Risk

New caterers often complain to me that they can't afford to buy insurance and pay the premiums. I tell them they can't afford not to. In fact you should budget for it from the start. Consider what would happen if your kitchen caught fire in the middle of party preparation. How would you replace equipment? Fulfill your contract? Insurance protects existing assets and provides a continuous future for your company.

Listed here are the essential types of insurance with which to start. Discuss these with your attorney. Then sound out several companies and agents about coverage and rates. Look for insurance companies that specialize in restaurants and caterers. A local chapter of the National Restaurant Association can help you with a referral list. Be aware that there are additional types of policies available to you as your business grows.

Two examples: Business interruption insurance covers your fixed costs and expenses if a fire shuts down your business. Salaries to employees, taxes, utilities, as well as the profits you are losing, also can be covered. There is mortgage insurance if you own your building and want to insure payment of the mortgage in the face of catastrophe.

Start-Up Coverage

If at first all your storage is at home, check to see if you can upgrade your existing tenant's or homeowner's property insurance. Get the broadest available coverage. This policy can cover fire losses, vandalism, wind damage, smoke damage, explosions, and even malicious mischief.

Product-Liability Insurance

Don't even think about serving food to the public without product-liability insurance protection. The coverage protects you and pays your client damages in the event that the food you serve is or becomes contaminated. Your company can even be sued for serving someone else's contaminated product. Know your purveyors and insist that their product is also insured.

What if a bride wants you to serve a wedding cake made by her best friend? The friend is going to make this cake in her home, she has no product insurance, no licensed and legal business, and no board of health permit. What do you do? You explain to the bride that she, personally, will have to sign a liability waiver with your company, giving up her rights and her guests'

Elements to Cover in a Catering Contract

1. Date and day of catering
2. Location of catering
3. Minimum guest count for menu pricing
4. Date of notification for final guest count
5. Exact time your catering work starts and ends
6. Fire-safety floor plan and seating arrangements
7. Final menu selection and price per person
8. Description of service and labor quotation
9. Staff schedule
10. Approximate additional costs/subcontractors
11. Deposit money and payment schedule for balance
12. Cancellation policy and refund of deposit
13. Anticipated total cost
14. Signatures

---

rights to any legal action against you in the event of food poisoning or contamination. Her other option, of course, is to buy her wedding cake from a licensed and insured bakery or from you.

Serving the public food is an enormous responsibility. It should never be taken lightly.

Public-Liability Insurance

Public-liability insurance covers injury to the public. A customer or client falls down during a party and gets hurt. You could be sued. You want to buy the biggest policy you can afford. Find out about purchasing one-day coverage for individual events involving unusual situations.

I once had a bride and groom arrive by helicopter. The owner of the property wanted additional coverage for them to land in his backyard. I couldn't blame him. My client paid for the day rider fee.

Workers' Compensation Insurance

This type of insurance covers *employees* in case of injury at work. Catering is a high-risk business. Kitchen work involves knives, fire, and heavy lifting. Chances of accidents are greater in this business than in libraries, say. Speak to an attorney to find out exactly what your financial and legal obligations are in your state.

In California it is illegal to operate any business with employees without worker's compensation insurance. Check with your state's industrial relations department to find out what requirements you must adhere to.

In every state, under common law, employers are required to provide employees with a safe place to work. They are also required to train employees to be competent and safe coworkers, to provide the safest tools for employees to handle, and to warn employees of existing dangers such as fumes from certain chemical cleaners or exposure to pesticides (poisons) on a continuous basis. If you fail as an employer to protect your employees, you are risking a lawsuit and damages.

Written Agreements and Contracts

With the first phone call to any client, you are creating a contract. Whether you want to put it in writing or not is your business, but, trust me, it's easier to keep track of the dimes and dollars involved in catering finances with a written agreement. A written contract is an enforceable document.

From my previous life as a real estate agent, I brought to my catering career my habit of documenting every conversation about business. In real estate you're taught "to get it in writing" because an oral contract will not hold up in court if a problem arises in closing a transaction. So, for me, it was natural to write down every detail of an upcoming event, making sure that all parties indicated their agreement by signing. When other caterers tell me they have never needed a contract, I assume they have not staged lavish, expensive parties or worked with corporate clients. A corporation planning an employee bash for 250 achievers or parents spending $25,000 on a wedding want to know what they have paid for and what they are going to get.

It makes no difference to me whether my client's bill is for $500 or $50,000; I want to provide everything as promised because I want my clients to feel they got their money's worth and to tell their friends about me. In return I need to know that my client will pay me what we agreed, that I will get the money on the dates we decided (the better to manage my cash flow), and that we both intend to do what we promised in good faith.

Take a look at the sample contract that follows on pages 60–67. Not only does it keep track of everything you need to remember and have promised, but it provides an entire script if you are new at selling and closing a deal. (Before you use it, however, be sure to run it by your attorney.)

Let's say you have had one or two conversations with a client and pitched your ideas over the phone or by fax. Write that information in the spaces provided. Start at the top. Fill in all the other blanks with your client. By the time you get to the signature at the end, this party is starting to take shape.

The more preparation and organization you put into party planning, the smoother it will run. By showing your client your business skills from the beginning, you are building a basis of trust, assurance, and professionalism.

Every contract decision in catering boils down to how much it will cost, so get this information right from the start. Put the costs in the contract and no one will be surprised later.

An example: A new client calls and says she can spend $30 per person. Does she mean on food alone? Or is she assuming that $30 will cover everything, including rentals, food, taxes, and staff? A good contract will make the point clear.

Contracts are made up of three parts: offer, acceptance, and consideration or money. Protect yourself and your clients by detailing these parts and the agreement between you.

Working with
Subcontractors or Suppliers

What happens if the fish that your purveyor supplies turns out to be tainted and your clients' guests get sick? Or if the disk jockey rigs up the stereo system in such a way that a guest trips over a cord and breaks a leg? So that you're not held responsible, insist that each supplier or subcontractor sign an agreement holding you harmless against any losses or claims made by your clients because of the suppliers' own negligence or oversight. I'm sure it doesn't surprise you to learn that you will want to consult an attorney for the appropriate language here.

In general it pays to make sure that the subcontractors you work with are licensed and insured and that any employees they send to work with you are covered by worker's compensation. After all, if it's the disc jockey himself who trips over the speaker cord and breaks a leg, you want his employer to take care of him.

Employees

When you started your home-based catering business, you became your own boss. As you take on larger or more complex parties, you might find it necessary to hire kitchen assistants, waiters, or bartenders to help you produce your events. Now you are someone else's boss. If this is your first time as a boss or manager, I offer a reading list (see page 75) geared to minimizing "people" problems and maximizing employee potential.

In my consulting business the biggest complaint I hear again and again is "I can't find any good helpers." Well, if party after party, year after year, you have the same problems with personnel, the real problem is you, not your help. You need to be a great manager to have a great staff.

Good management practices create good employees. Think

Sample Contract

Client name _____

Title _____

Company _____

Address _____

City/State/Zip _____

Event date _____

Start time _____ End time _____

Guest count _____ Minimum guarantee _____

Final count _____ By date _____

We request the final guest count and payment balance three days before your event. Menu price (per person) is based on your minimum guest count. If the minimum count goes down, we may have to reprice your menu. If your count goes up after you have given us the final count, we will be happy to try to accommodate you as best we can.

Location _____

Contact name _____   Telephone _____

Directions _____   Travel time _____

Location rules/restrictions _____

_____

Special insurance requirements _____   Cost _____

Tent _____   Permits required _____

Cost $ _____

Does the location provide for day deliveries the day before the event and for early staff arrival?

_____

Circle the location features that apply:

Parking available/Staff changing room/Bathrooms

Security service _____

Cost $ _____

Type of Event _____

Theme/Decor _____

Cost $ _____

[Floor plan/party layout design]

Table size _____ Number of chairs _____

Rentals and linens quotation $ _____

Sizes _____

Date ordered _____ Date confirmed _____

Special equipment _____

Cost $ _____

Menu (based on the minimum guarantee) _____

Time each course will be served _____

Price per person $ _____ Disposables per person $ _____

Bar and wine selections _____

Price per person $ _____ Bar setup/Supplies $ _____

Soft drinks and water $ _____

Type of service _____

Special instructions _____

Number of staff _____

Party managers _____   Chefs _____

Waiters _____   Bartenders _____

Kitchen assistants _____   Delivery driver _____

Labor quotation $ _____

Uniforms _____

Subcontractors

Florist _____   Parking valet _____

Telephone _____   Telephone _____

Federal ID number _____   Federal ID number _____

Certificate of insurance _____   Certificate of insurance _____

Signed loss and damage waiver on file _____   Signed loss and damage waiver on file _____

Photographer _____

Telephone _____

Federal ID number _____

Certificate of insurance _____

Signed loss and damage waiver on file _____

Entertainment _____

Telephone _____

Federal ID number _____

Certificate of insurance _____

Signed loss and damage waiver on file _____

In case of guest overages:

Authorized credit card number/approved limit _____ $ _____

Anticipated total cost: $ _____

15% service charge* $ _____

8¼% state sales tax $ _____

Grand total $ _____

Upon acceptance we require a 50% deposit of the entire bill

Deposit $ _____

Balance due $ _____ Date _____

*Optional for small parties or parties where all you do is drop off the food, but highly recommended for parties of any complexity. See chapter 5 for more information on pricing goods and services.

Caterer shall not be liable for any damage in the event that performance shall be delayed or prevented by fire, flood, riot, strike, labor dispute, or act of God. Caterer reserves the right to subcontract any or all of its obligations hereunder.

Should customer cancel the event for any reason whatsoever, customer shall be liable for all out-of-pocket costs sustained by the caterer.

Caterer does not assume or accept any responsibility for damages to the location, loss of personal articles, or broken or unreturned rentals.

Accepted by _____   Date _____

Caterer _____

about your own personality and what makes you work to your full potential. Think about jobs that you adored or disliked and bosses that you hated or respected. What were important issues to you when you were an employee? Your own work record offers you insights into human behavior and guidelines to be the kind of boss you respect.

Here are some points to keep in mind as you work toward building a winning team:

- Are you providing your employees with everything they need to do the job well (equipment, supplies, etc.)?
- Have you made your expectations clear to your employees (arrive on time, wear clean uniforms, be courteous to guests, etc.)?
- Have you made job duties clear to all employees (roll silver in napkins, uncork wine, zest lemon peels, assemble dessert trays, etc.)?
- Do you treat your employees with courtesy and respect?
- Do you encourage comments and suggestions from your employees? (Do you use their ideas when they're better than yours?)
- Do you give employees an honest assessment of their performance in a positive way (encouragement, positive reinforcement)?
- Do you offer praise and compliments when deserved?
- Do you apologize when an apology is owed?
- Do you thank your employees for the talent and support they bring to the team?
- Do you solicit an evaluation of *your* performance from your employees?
- Do you pay your employees promptly?

In your successful catering company, a shared vision or team spirit must prevail. All good teams need a coach or strong leader who sets the tone and policy.

Hiring Versus Leasing Employees

Hiring employees can be an exercise in paperwork, even if you use them only occasionally. You need to think about payroll taxes, social security taxes, unemployment insurance, and worker's compensation. A reasonable alternative for the home-based caterer is to use employment services that send out temps. Here in Los Angeles several personnel services have chefs, waiters, and bus boys on tap. You determine the size of the staff you need, and the company sends them out in uniform. You pay an hourly fee for each. The fee is higher than what you'd pay if you hired each person directly, but you write just one check to the personnel company and it handles the payroll, employee taxes, and worker's compensation. Using this kind of service as you grow may well save you cash. It will certainly save the time you'd otherwise have to spend interviewing people and puzzling over mounds of paperwork.

Employees Versus Independent Contractors

I happen to prefer hiring my own employees, and I've perfected a system for screening them, as you'll see later in this chapter. Going to the extra trouble is worth it to me because it's the best way I know to build team spirit. You may end up feeling the same way. If so, know that if you hire waiters, bartenders, kitchen help, or other help yourself, even on a very occasional basis, it's not a good idea to try to avoid paying taxes by claiming that they're independent contractors. For someone to qualify as an independent contractor, he or she must work without supervision, supply his or her own materials, be considered an expert in his or her field, and work at his or her own pace. Once you tell someone when and where to show up and how long to work, that person is an employee. Talk with your attorney and your accountant for more information about exactly what your obligations are.

Labor Practices

You should also contact your local division of industrial relations (probably listed under your state in the phone book) and ask a representative to send you a copy of the regulations governing catering in your area. In California, for example, you'd call the Industrial Welfare Commission and ask for a copy of

Wages, Hours and Working Conditions in the Public House-keeping Industry.

As an owner/employer you need to be aware of the current minimum wage. You need to pay for every hour worked by an employee. You have to know how many consecutive hours and days determine overtime pay. You have to know how many breaks an employee is entitled to in one shift and when an employee is entitled to a meal and rest facilities.

You need to keep a copy of these orders available for any employee or post a copy where it is easy for employees to read.

Each person you hire to help run your business goes out into the marketplace and is a reflection of you. Choose your help carefully. In chapter 2 we discussed hiring family and friends. Well, as your business grows, you will want to develop a larger network from which to choose.

There are no shortcuts to building a terrific team. It takes time to interview and get to know a prospective employee. You spend valuable time and money to create a staff to help you run your business efficiently.

Tip: Never hire anyone you haven't interviewed at least three times. You only start to see the person behind the interview facade the third time.

Applications/Job Interviews

Standard employment applications are available in stationery stores, or you can call your local restaurant association. State and federal laws govern questions that you can legally ask job applicants.

On pages 72–73 is an example of an application I adapted after years of experience. I learned to ask pertinent questions about food-related talents. Not only does it save me time in the first interview, but it gives me a feel for the applicant's talent and expresses my high expectations at the very beginning.

After prospective employees have filled out the application, start the interview process. Following are some questions you might want to ask:

1. Would you be interested in working for me in a professional relationship as a paid employee?

2. Will you and I be able to be honest and up-front with each other?
3. I respect your opinion. I'd like your input about how you see me as a manager. After we have worked our first event, would you be willing to give me such an evaluation?
4. What are your strongest attributes?
5. Your weakest?
6. I am developing a party-procedure list for all my employees. I want your honest reaction. We need to make another appointment to go over it. When would be convenient for you?
7. What kind of referral do you expect from your last boss?
8. Do you have any concerns about our working together?
9. I've written out a job description for you. After you've read it, please initial it and ask me any questions you might have.
10. Why are you applying for this job?
11. I start all employees at $_____ per hour. After three parties we meet again to discuss pay. Does this suit you?
12. (optional) Let me tell you why, as a friend or family member, I would like you to work for me.

Job Descriptions/Policy Manuals

Once you have hired someone, make it easy on yourself and your employee. Write out a job description and have the person read it. Then both of you edit it. When the two of you have established a comfortable range of job responsibilities, explain that you will use this piece of paper as a tool to help measure job performance and to use as a basis for raises.

Sample Job Description for Servers

General duties and responsibilities:
- set up tables and chairs
- put down table linens
- set tables
- put out salt and pepper shakers
- keep ashtrays emptied
- keep water glasses filled
- serve courses
- bus tables between each course
- serve wine/take drink orders
- collect and count table linens
- break down tables and chairs

Application for Employment

Date _____

Job you are applying for _____

Social Security Number _____   Telephone _____

Name _____

Address _____

Employment history (food service only) _____

_____

_____

List three references with phone numbers:

_____

_____

_____

Days and times you are available for work:

Weekdays _____ a.m. or p.m.   Weekends _____ a.m. or p.m.

Please answer and evaluate yourself with the following: Average = A   Good = B   Excellent = E

Do you have experience opening champagne or wine? _____ Do you know buffet service? _____

French service? _____ Russian service? _____

(French or English service is the presentation of each course plate; Russian service is platters served person to person by the waiters.)

Do you know how to carry a waiter's tray? _____ Do you know how to pass appetizers? _____

Do you have busing experience? _____ Do you have food-preparation experience? _____

Do you know how to cut a wedding cake? _____ Do you know how to set up a buffet ? _____

Do you know how to carve meat on a buffet? Have you ever done it? _____

Do you have food-garnishing skills? _____

Tell me in a paragraph about any other skills that you have and why you think they would be helpful in a catering job. _____

_____

_____

Please answer: If you saw another employee stealing from me or my client, what would you do?

A written job description offers a set of boundaries and guidelines that should answer any questions a new employee has and helps eliminate mistakes. New bosses are often guilty of the "if-only-my-employees-could-read-my-mind syndrome." Remember that you hired a waiter, not a psychic.

In addition, if you as an employer are not satisfied with your employee's job performance, a job description serves as a written reference to amend or document grounds for warnings, suspension, or termination.

When you have decided what kind of behavior you expect from all your employees, regardless of their position or job description, tell them. Write your policies down. Give everyone a copy. Have each employee initial them. With these policies in writing, employees are at much less risk of disappointing you or themselves.

As a matter of good record keeping, prepare folders for each employee. You will need to document every promotion, pay change, tax change, or change of address made when someone is in your employ. The employee folder is open to the employee for inspection at any time. Letters of recommendation or a complaint should also be put there.

Where to Look for Great Staff

1. Other caterers
2. Waiters at your favorite café
3. Local culinary students from hospitality programs
4. Personnel directors of hotels or conference centers for applications they've received but didn't use
5. Theater or performance groups (actors make great waiters)
6. Personnel service agencies
7. Hospitals or rest-home kitchen employees
8. City or county employees for moonlighting on weekends
9. Hungry college kids
10. Women who love to cook and entertain but have never had a job outside the home

Employee policies

1. You are responsible for your own clean, pressed uniform.
2. Keep shoulder-length hair tied back at all times.
3. Jewelry should be kept to a minimum. Small stud earrings requested if your ears are pierced.
4. No political badges
5. Black socks and shoes only
6. Clean, short, lightly polished fingernails
7. No chewing gum or smoking on the floor of the party
8. There is no excuse for being late.
9. No eating or drinking except at scheduled breaks—never on the floor of the party
10. No drugs or alcohol before or during your shift
11. No more than two waiters congregating on the floor of the party
12. No employees are allowed to take any food or beverages off the property.

Becoming a Great Manager Booklist

The One Minute Manager, Kenneth H. Blanchard and Spencer Johnson, M.D. (Berkley Books, 1981).

Putting the One Minute Manager to Work, Kenneth H. Blanchard and Robert Lorber, Ph.D. (Berkley Books, 1984).

How to Win Friends and Influence People, Dale Carnegie (S & S Trade, 1936).

How to Make Meetings Work, Michael Doyle & David Strauss (Jove Publishers, 1976).

13 Fatal Errors Managers Make, How You Can Avoid Them, W. Stephen Brown (Berkley Books, 1985).

Managing Behavior on the Job, Paul L. Brown (Wiley & Sons, Inc., 1982).

5

Setting Prices, Estimating Quantities, and Writing Proposals

The biggest mistake most new caterers make is underpricing the food they sell. They get into this habit because they are used to cooking for family and friends for free and without worrying about labor costs or overhead. Any profit seems grand if you see food as your only expense.

Of course food *isn't* your only expense; even if you're not shouldering the expenses of an elaborate storefront and a permanent staff of six, you need to factor in your time and your labor when pricing menus. But that's not all. Before you arrive at a final price for a party, you also need to take into account the staff costs; price of flowers, decor, and entertainment; the cost of supplies; and your overhead.

How to Price Your First Menus

Since many caterers start their business the day they land their first job, they don't really have enough experience to know how much it costs or how long it takes to make various dishes. The more catering you do, the faster you will become at menu pricing and food production. Time is your earning power. You must learn to measure it and charge accordingly. The following information will help you do just that.

The cardinal rule of accurate pricing is simple: Use a calculator and fill out a menu pricing form (see page 81) for every item.

Don't guess on your menu prices. Don't assume you know how much products cost without verifying the prices with your purveyors. Prices on products change from season to season, week to week. Do your calculations carefully. Recalculate and, if necessary, reprice your menus every three months. Your investment in time will pay you back in dollars.

For your first menus it's wise to choose six different themes to show versatility. One might be an American Barbecue, another your fabulous fried chicken billed as a Southern Sunday Dinner, another your Italian Pasta Collection, another a Cajun Celebration, and so on. Be sure the menus reflect your niche and the research you did on your competition. To control costs and make life easier in your kitchen, try to sell these complete menus (as opposed to specific dishes) whenever possible. Remember that perfect menus are flavorful, colorful, nutritionally balanced, varied enough to appeal to a wide range of tastes, and in step with current food trends.

It is also smart to add a disclaimer to the bottom of your menus: "All items and products subject to availability."

When it comes to pricing your menus, it doesn't matter if they're for complete dinners, buffets, deli planners, or drop-off picnic lunches—the process is the same. Calculate every menu price per person, and make it clear when you quote the price to your client that it is for food only. Party wait staff, decor, soft drinks, disposables, and rentals are all separate costs.

Don't take the shortcut of pricing your menus to match or beat your competition. Their prices don't tell you whether they're making any money. You want to compete, but you also want to be profitable.

Here's what is involved in setting menu prices:
- Analyze your food costs. List every ingredient in the dish on

Sample Menu Themes

Day at the Circus
Hamburgers • Corn dogs • Peanuts • Popcorn • Cotton candy
Carrot curls • Animal crackers • Ice-cream bars

South of France Picnic
Red potato salad • Rare roast beef with Dijon mustard
Baguettes with sweet butter • Marinated haricots verts in champagne-shallot vinaigrette

Western Roundup
Three-alarm turkey chili with corn bread • Beef stew • Mashed yams
Roasted potatoes • Garden vegetable salad

Edge of Thailand
Chicken satay with peanut sauce • Spring rolls • Cucumber salad
Pad thai noodles • Sizzling rice soup • Sautéed lobster in black beans

Chinese Marketplace
Szechuan chicken • Black mushrooms and beef stir-fry • Shui mai
Potstickers • Shrimp fried rice • Sautéed vegetables

Viennese Dessert Buffet
Bite-sized napoleons • Cream puffs • Éclairs • Linzer tortes
Chocolate truffles • Orange Florentine cookies

South American Fiesta
Pork empanadas • Carne asada • Tamales • Soft chicken tacos
Grilled vegetables • Flan

Rockin' Fifties Soda Bar
Hot fudge sundaes • Banana splits • Root beer floats • Egg creams
Strawberry shakes

Anniversary Dinner Plate

New York steak, 10 ounces @ $6.95 per pound	=	$4.40
Baked potato, 5 ounces @ 69 cents per pound	=	$ .25
Green beans, 4 ounces @ 89 cents per pound	=	$ .24
Sautéed mushrooms, 6 ounces @ $1.89 per pound	=	$ .72
Butter, 3 ounces @ $2.00 per pound	=	$ .39
Sour cream, 3 ounces @ $1.89 per pound	=	$ .36
Condiments: olive oil, spices, fresh garlic		$ .40
	Total costs:	$6.76

Calculate: $6.76 divided by 34 percent food cost = approximately $20.
$6.76 divided by 28% food cost = approximately $24. That's your target range.

If your food cost percentage is 34 percent, that means you're spending 34 cents out of every dollar on food, which leaves you 66 cents for kitchen labor (about 15 percent), overhead (variable based on monthly sales—see chapter 7), and profit.

Sample Menu Item Pricing Form

Menu Item _____ Date _____

(1) Ingredients	(2) Unit	(3) Unit Cost	(4) Portion	(5) Portion Cost
		$		$
		$		$
		$		$
		$		$
		$		$

Cooking condiments $ _____

Total cost $ _____

Desired food cost percentage _____ %

Menu price $ _____

Gross profit (menu price minus food cost) $ _____

your menu pricing form. Determine the amount you are going to serve per portion and the exact cost of that amount. Add up the total cost for each dish.

- Divide the total cost by your target food cost percentage to arrive at a price. In order to ensure profit, I like my food cost to run between 28 and 34 percent of my menu price, although I've been known to get it down to 22 percent.

Start by breaking each item down into the proper number of ounces per serving. (To arrive at a per-ounce cost, divide the price per pound by 16 ounces.)

After pricing every menu you design, document the individual dishes with recipe cards. If you wish, you can buy computer programs that multiply recipes for whatever size yield you need. You can also buy catering software to help you in the beginning with food cost percentages and estimating food quantities. See sidebar on page 85.

For the long term growth of your reputation, it's important to be able to duplicate every product consistently so that you can guarantee quality standards job after job. The busier you get, the likelier it is you'll delegate preparation tasks to others. Just make sure that you test your recipes yourself before you pass them on.

For example, my partner and I were asked to make fifty lemon bundt cakes for another caterer. (We priced each cake at $8.50 after dividing the $1.89 raw product cost by our target food cost percentage of 24 percent.) Because we only owned ten bundt pans, we multiplied the recipe by ten and decided to bake five batches. After the first batch, we knew the conversions were correct, and we were able to leave the recipe card with a prep cook to make the remaining forty cakes. I continued making cold calls on the phone, and my partner worked on the corporate lunch we had scheduled for the next day.

Calculating Your Kitchen Labor

You'll need to keep track of the number of hours it takes you or someone you hire to shop and prepare any food in your kitchen. The more complicated the plate, the higher the labor, and the higher the sales price.

Chart A

Estimated shopping and kitchen prep time

Guest count: 50 to 100

Type of Work	Estimated Hours
Continental breakfast	1½
Cheese/crudités platters	2
Box lunches	3½
Three passed hors d'oeuvres	4
Appetizer stations	6
Two entrées	6
Plated dinner service	6–7

The higher the guest count, the lower your kitchen labor percentage (wages divided by sales price) is likely to be. Simply put, you can fix food for a hundred guests in the same amount of time it takes you to fix food for fifty guests. (See Chart A above).

Whether you're cooking a menu or a single dish, document on the recipe card or your menu pricing form the amount of time it takes, the exact yield, and the level of expertise it takes to produce. If you find that your labor costs are amounting to more than 15 percent of the menu price, consider raising your prices—or choose simpler recipes.

How to Estimate the Right Food Quantities

The second most common problem for the new caterer is either making too much food or not enough. This can be as deadly to your business as underpricing your menu.

Many factors play into the amount of food you need to allow for each guest. For years I have managed to make just the right amount of food party after party by taking the following factors into account.

The Age Group of the Guests

The older a group is, the less they tend to eat. Envision the amount of food that athletic, teenaged boys might eat in an afternoon compared with the amount that a group of retired women might consume.

The Guests' Life-style

Will the guests be primarily singles or couples? Singles usually come to a party thrilled to be getting a home-cooked (and free) meal. Couples are likelier to have food in their refrigerator, especially if they have kids. As a result, couples eat less.

The Style of the Party

Will people be seated comfortably at tables? Or will the party be a stand-up buffet in a packed room where it's impossible to elbow your way back for seconds?

Rule of thumb: For a buffet, plan to bring one-and-a-half times the amount of portions per guest of each menu item. For a sit-down meal bring 10 percent more than the guest count (and know that guests eat twice as much bread at a sit-down dinner).

Time of Party

Is the party scheduled for a time normally associated with a full-fledged meal? Guests may not eat before they come, in which case they'll be starving! Or will it be in the middle of the afternoon, when guests will already have eaten? In the latter case, you can probably get away with serving less food.

Computer Programs for Caterers

A program called *Micro Cookbook* by Pinpoint Publishing, P.O. Box 1359, Glen Ellen, CA 95442 (707–523–0400), stores your recipes, prints them on 3 x 5 cards, automatically adjusts and recalculates the ingredients for greater or fewer portions, and provides information on nutritional content. It can also perform searches for recipes with specific ingredients so that you can satisfy clients who want, say, something with feta cheese and red bell pepper in it. The program comes complete with 350 recipes, and you can add your own. You can even tell the program what you have left in your refrigerator and it will come up with some recipes for you!

Recipe Writer Pro, Sales Analysis Pro, and *Inventory Pro* are excellent programs published by At-Your-Service Software, Inc., 450 Bronxville Road, Bronxville, NY 10708 (914–337–9030). Sales Analysis Pro works alone or with the other two programs to track your best-selling items. It also calculates your average food cost percentage over a given period and shows you which food items are selling and which are dropping. In addition it tracks the profitability of what you sell.

Inventory Pro tracks your inventory and helps you maintain an accurate count of the products you have in stock.

Recipe Writer Pro will pay for itself after your first three parties. As you would expect, it does quantity conversions and calculates your food cost and profit margin per plate and per ingredient. (Aren't you relieved that you don't have to calculate everything by hand?) The program also offers ingredient searches, recipe writing, and purchasing information. You can even store notes about individual clients' needs and food preferences.

Nature of the Party

You need to know the guests' motivation for being at the affair. Is it a business lunch where workers only want to show their faces and leave? In that case they may well skip dessert. Or is it a wedding—say an Italian wedding like mine, where the guests ate for three hours, took a break, and then went back to work on the buffet some more?

Client's Concern about Running Out of Food

I have had clients express so much concern that they'll run out of food that I have brought backup product to relieve their fears. I sell it to them with the understanding that I probably won't serve it. They can have it for the next day, with reheating instructions, but it is not my policy to refund any money.

Say that you're hired to put on a fiftieth wedding anniversary party (see the anniversary menu on page 80). The first thing you should ask your client is the age group of the guests. If you know that all ages will be represented, make the portions average size. If you find out that most of the guests will be in their seventies, cut down the steak portion to seven ounces. In my experience older people eat smaller portions, drink very little, prefer decaffeinated coffee, leave before it gets dark, and want to take dessert home with them. (Be sure to bring foil or extra paper plates and napkins so that they can wrap the desserts.)

On the other hand, say that you find out the majority of guests at the anniversary party are the couple's grandchildren and their friends from college. Not only can college boys devour a sixteen-ounce steak standing up, they'll want to wash it down with plenty of beer and tequila shooters. The party takes on a different tone entirely.

When I figure portions, at the end of my calculations, I up them 10 percent to cover my employees and an extra guest or two. (In this part of the world, it's understood that staff will have a chance to eat once they've served the guests.) If a client orders an extravagant entrée like live lobster from Maine or extra-thick lamb chops, the food cost is too high to buy extra portions "on spec." Instead I state in the proposal that I'll do my best to accommodate last-minute guest increases, but if the guest count grows in the last twenty-four hours before the party, the menu price might well increase, because I will be scurrying around to find comparable lobster and lamb chops retail at the last minute (I may even have to pay someone to go shopping for me). Of course, with a menu of Maine lobster or lamb chops, I don't expect to have my staff eat the leftovers—instead, I bring them chicken breasts or pasta.

Quoting Other Party Costs

If you're to fill out a contract for each party, as I recommended in chapter 4, you'll want to make sure you know how to quote the other costs involved.

Estimating Wait Staff

Five important factors determine how much help you'll need to hire for any job or party. Answer these questions with the information you have gathered from your client, from visiting the location, and from working with your budget worksheet.
1. How far is the party from where you park and off-load?
2. What kind of menu and what type of service is required?
3. What ratio of help to guests will your clients pay for?
4. How many stories are there at the location?
5. Are you using china and glasses or plastic disposables?

Disposables

The amount of paper and plastic products, foil pans, garbage bags, and cans of Sterno you use at each party will astound you, but you can pass on the cost of these items directly to your client.

I ask either my rental company (which sells disposables by the case) or a wholesale party goods store to give me a price quotation, which I mark up by 50 percent. To arrive at a per

Chart B		
Wait staff		
Type of Party	Guest Count	Staff
Cocktails	1–100	1 bartender
Cocktails with appetizers	1–100	1 bartender 1 waiter
Self-serve buffet	1–100	3 waiters 1 chef
Sit-down dinner	1–20	1 waiter/1 buser 1 chef

person cost, I divide this number by how many people will be at the party.

Floral, Decor, and Subcontractors' Services

Remember that any extra services your clients request are just that—extras. Musicians, florists, specialty desserts, or decor are services you have the expertise to provide. It takes more of your time to coordinate this kind of party or event, so you charge for it.

It's standard in the industry for a caterer to add on an additional 10 to 20 percent to the subcontractors' invoices. This markup covers the phone calls, paperwork, and time you spend organizing.

The Art of Bidding and Writing a Proposal

As a caterer you will often be called on to write proposals and bid for jobs. In your proposals you will describe your menu, name your price, explain your schedule of payment, and enclose a cover letter telling the client why he or she should choose you. Creative, well-written proposals are perhaps the best sales tools around. Call or sit down with your client and ask him or her the following questions to elicit the information you need. Write down the answers on a client inquiry sheet that you design yourself. In this way you'll have a report of what your client wants and what you suggested even if it takes your client three months to decide.

1. Am I the only caterer with whom you are working? If not, whom else are you approaching? I'd like to know my competition.

2. Are you giving each caterer the same budget? If not, why? (Sometimes a company's reputation precedes it. A client may hear you are cheaper and wants to prove it.)

3. For whom is the party being given? Is it social or corporate? What is its purpose?

4. What are the date and time of the party? (Remember that seasons and time of day dictate food choices and quantities. Holidays mean different pay scales for staff and may interfere with delivery of produce and props.)

5. Where will the party be held? (You will want to look at kitchen facilities at that location and also determine what types of rentals may be needed. Be sure to get the name and phone number of someone at the location.)

6. What's your budget? (Needless to say, the answer to this question determines your whole approach and should allow you to gauge whether the client is realistic or asking you to spin your wheels.)

7. What sort of party do you have in mind? Casual or elegant? Cocktail or buffet? Sit-down dinner? Exhibition cooking with food stations? Dessert only?

8. What do you want the party to look like? Do you have a color scheme in mind? Have you selected invitations yet? (Suggest ideas and current trends. If you are taking down this information over the phone, make an appointment to

review your portfolio of party pictures with the client. You will want to be able to ballpark both design and floral costs.)

9. What sort of menu do you have in mind? (Try to sell a menu you do well and you know is profitable. If you have another party the same day or week, try to sell the same menu to save food and minimize labor costs.)

Make your proposals thorough and precise. If the client is nervous about entertaining or hiring you, this detailed party plan will put him or her at ease.

Your proposal may have to outshine the bids of the older, more established caterers, so write it as though the client has never been to a party and knows nothing about you and your fresh, fabulous food or your impeccable eye for detail.

Your bag of tricks has to include glowing prose. Even if it's only cheese and crackers, make it the most interesting cheese you ever bought. Talk about where the cheese comes from. What kind of special crackers are they? Aim for something like this: "Wooden crock of aged English Stilton surrounded by ripe Bosc pear slices, fresh mint, red grapes, toasted baguette rounds, whole-wheat crackers, and graham biscuits served on antique silver trays with red brocade linen."

Don't fall into the trap of thinking you won't be able to compete with the big guys. Many home-based caterers or even part-time caterers are selected over established companies on the merits of a well-written proposal.

Now try the exercise I give students in my catering classes:

The dean of the film school at a local university calls you and tells you that he wants to throw a party to fete the winners in a student film competition. He tells you that he's getting bids from two other caterers and that all three of you have worked for the university before. If you're interested in doing the party, you'll need to fax him your proposal within three hours, as his committee meeting is early the next morning.

The dean prefers to give you carte blanche on decor and menu so long as you stay within his budget of $5,000. To round out the picture, you elicit the following information from him:

Name of party: THE BRIGHT NEW STARS OF
TOMORROW
Date: Monday, November 15, 7–10 p.m.
Location: Director's Guild, Hollywood (location
donated)
Guest Count: 500 to 600 people
Guest Profile: Students, instructors, patrons, and
celebrity alumni
Budget: $5,000 plus tax

Here's the actual proposal I wrote when the dean of the
UCLA film school came to me with just such a party in mind:

Denise Vivaldo
Martin-Vivaldo Party Planners

October 15

Dear Dean,
Thanks for calling Martin-Vivaldo Party Planners for a
proposal to cater The Bright New Stars of Tomorrow. The enclosed proposal was designed to suit your needs and please
your guests.

Budget: I understand that the university has $5,000 for
this party and not a penny more. We need to establish a maximum guest count. Some 500 people for $5,000 is $10 per person. If this count goes up, you will need to pay me an
additional $10 per person. For this amount Martin-Vivaldo
Party Planners will provide setup, breakdown by my staff,
rentals and display pieces, decor, and food. You will provide
students to help my waiters. You said that the wine, water,
and ice are being donated. Would you like an estimate of the
quantity needed?
Usually about two-thirds of the guests invited will attend.
Ask guests to RSVP by the Thursday before.

Menu: We talked about cheese and crackers to go with
the wine. Since the party is after dinner, I'd like the menu to
include a variety of cookies, brownies, lemon bars, and dessert

cheeses. My chef will garnish the display with red and green grape garlands and whole strawberries. Do you want coffee and tea service?

Time: Your invitation should ask guests to arrive on time at 6:45 P.M. Guests will be escorted directly to the screening rooms by student filmmakers. The three shorts will end at about 8:30 P.M.

My staff will be in place to open the wine bar and food stations at 8:15 P.M. The double doors to the party room will be open as the guests descend the stairway. Portable spotlights will guide them to the door, compliments of the theater art department.

You might want to reconsider your rule of "no breaks during the screening." I know you hope to keep on schedule without breaks, but if you don't have them, the ladies' rest rooms will be jammed between 8:30 and 8:45 P.M.

It would be nice to have two of your department staff volunteer to be bathroom monitors (replace tissue, wipe counters, and so forth). I admit this is not a glamorous job, but it is essential.

Layout: As the guests walk in, drinks will be on three 8-foot-long tables draped in white linen with black metallic overlays. The wine and water will already be poured by your volunteer wait staff. Pouring wine and water ahead of time makes it easy for guests to pick up a glass and cocktail napkin on the way to the buffet tables.

Two separate but identical serpentine (S-shaped banquet tables) food displays, each 16 feet long, will be placed perpendicular to the windows to make a dramatic statement. Besides giving guests room both to eat and to socialize, the placement of the buffet allows maximum flow.

Theme and Decor: I called the film historian on campus and asked if I might borrow props. She is happy to oblige with five miniature replicas of movie cameras. I also envision sparkling gold stars floating from the ceiling, stacks of antique tin film canisters, the camera replicas, and ribbons of film.

My three waiters will wear white tuxedo shirts, black slacks or skirts, and gold bow ties.

You might like the envelopes of your invitations to be sealed with small gold stars.

Parking: Please give me the name of the valet parking service you normally hire. Valet service must arrive at 6:30 P.M. Dress is black-and-white formal attire.

Location: I have called the manager of the Director's Guild, who faxed me the location guidelines. My company meets all the insurance requirements. I asked for a floor plan of the lobby, kitchen, and party areas.

Payment: We request 50 percent ($2,500) of the payment upon acceptance of this proposal. The balance, $2,500, will be due three days before the event.

Don't hesitate to call me with questions or changes. I look forward to hearing from you. Thank you again for thinking of Martin-Vivaldo Party Planners.

Very truly yours,
Denise Vivaldo

How to Stay Profitable When You're Working with a Fixed Price

You may find, as I did with this party, that a client prefers to give you a fixed price. Don't agree to take the party on until you've determined that you can do it profitably.

On page 94 you'll find the budget worksheet I filled out before writing the above proposal. This helped me decide whether to take the job or not.

A budget worksheet gives you the financial parameters you

Dean's Party Budget Worksheet

Food	$1,112.00
Beverage	(to be supplied by client)
Labor: kitchen	$80.00
setup/site	$342.00
Rentals	$201.00
Decor	$100.00
Facility rental	(waived)
Transportation	$75.00
Disposables	$100.00
Additional labor	
Proposal hours	$96.00
Unpacking and cleanup labor	$160.00
Total estimated costs:	**$2,094.00**
Income	$5,000.00
Gross profit	$2,906.00
Overhead (15 percent)*	–$435.90
Net profit	**$2,570.10**

*See chapter 7 for information on calculating your overhead percentage.

need to stick to if a given job is to be profitable. It forces you to estimate every last expense in advance so that you know exactly what you're getting into.

My advice is to get right to the budget when discussing a job with a prospective client. I believe that being honest and not wasting my time or the client's shows how professional I am. Your budget worksheet should help you avoid making promises you can't afford. Often a client doesn't want to pay as much as you want to spend. If you have your entire budget worked out, you'll be in a much better position to come up with a creative solution that meets both your needs and those of your client.

Remember: Budget worksheets are only for your use; they're not something you show a prospective client. The amount of money you make is your business.

Two days after I faxed the proposal, the dean called to say that we got the job. Except for the actual day of the event, most of our work was done. We were happy to accept. By working with a budget worksheet, you too can eliminate surprises and enable yourself to plan cash flow, profit, and your future.

Closing the Deal

Now that you know how to set prices and write a proposal, it's time to learn a few tricks about closing catering deals.

1. *Sometimes it pays to really stand out from the crowd.* Good catering is not so different from good theater—in both you create an effect. In my town caterers outdo themselves to come up with creative ways to present their proposals. One caterer I know recently told me how she submitted a proposal for the film premiere of *Charlie,* a film based on the life of Charlie Chaplin: She arrived hopelessly caught up in film with the proposal speared on the end of her cane. She got the job. You don't have to be a wild extrovert to succeed at this. Another home-based caterer I know convinced an Italian airline to serve her cookies on board by sending them a proposal, hand written in calligraphy, that was tucked into a basket shaped like a boot. The basket was stuffed with her cookies and wrapped in the colors of the Italian flag.

2. *Be firm but flexible.* Set the business ground rules about deposit money and guest guarantees, but be ready for changes from clients. After reading a proposal a client may be excited about working with you but may want to go in another direction entirely. Be prepared for changes, and you'll be able to take them in stride.

3. *Have a backup plan ready.* Clients like to think that they have options. For instance, one client decided out of the

Menu Analysis

Menu portion per guest	Cost	Quantities:		
1 chocolate brownie	$ .45	brownies	500	pieces
3.2 ounces whole grapes	$ .16	grapes	100	pounds
1.72 whole strawberries	$ .31	strawberries	6	flats
1 lemon bar	$ .55	lemon bars	500	
1 oatmeal raisin cookie	$ .25	oatmeal raisin cookies	500	
1 orange zest cookie	$ .25	orange zest cookies	500	
1 graham cracker biscuit	$ .04	graham cracker biscuits	576	
½ ounce whipped raspberry cream cheese	$ .065	raspberry cream cheese	6	pounds
1 taste of warm Brie with toasted almonds	$ .142	Brie	6	(1 kilo each)
		nuts	3	pounds
1 piece of baguette	$ .019	baguettes	20	
Total	**$2.24**			

Labor: By purchasing brownies and lemon bars from same bakery, I can get a good deal. Leaves me only the cookies (purchase frozen dough) to bake, grapes to wash and put back in box, strawberries to wipe with damp cloth. I also need to chop nuts, slice baguettes, whip cream-cheese mixture.

Kitchen prep:	cook—8 hrs. x $10.00	= $80.00
Setup/site:	waiters—15 hrs. x $10.00	= $150.00
	chef—8 hrs. x $12.00	= $96.00
	party manager—4 hrs. x $24.00	= $96.00
Proposal fee:	4 hrs. x $24.00	= $96.00
	Total labor costs:	**$528.00**

Rentals:

6	8-ft. tables @ $13.50	= $81.00
	12 banquet cloths x $10.00	= $120.00
	Total:	**$201.00**

Decor: Free from university. The archives historian will deliver to Director's Guild. Film cans and film are free from studio near my house. Black metallic overcloths cost about $200 new. This is the third time I have sold this decor this year. I charge $100 and pick up some profit.

Transportation: Van rental (including insurance, tax, and gas)
| **Total:** | $75.00 |

Disposables: Garbage-bag liners, 1,000 cocktail napkins, plastic wrap, 600 5-inch paper plates, 100 plastic knives for Brie, aluminum pans to carry leftovers home, 750 small plastic cups no bigger than 5 ounces.
| **Total cost:** | **$100.00** |

blue that she didn't want a three-piece band. I quickly came up with the cost of a disc jockey and suggested that she allocate the money she saved to an ice-cream sundae bar. She appreciated how quickly I was able to suggest an alternative—and she loved the idea of a sundae bar.

4. *Make good use of photographs, letters of recommendation, and videos.* Show your client what you can do for him or her with visual presentation. A dazzling portfolio or short video of a recent party is proof positive that you do a good job. You should also make sure that you ask satisfied clients for written recommendations. Do it right after the party when the client is flushed with success. You'll get a great letter that you can use to wow prospective clients.

5. *No matter what happens, be professional: Never knock your competition.* I've already told you to ask clients what other caterers they're considering. Once you know, don't knock the competition. Instead compliment the client for selecting the best caterers in town. Then prove to her that you'll suit her best.

6

Sales and Marketing
Selling Yourself and Your Company

It doesn't matter how great a caterer you are if only a handful of people know it. Creating an image for yourself and telling the world about it is what marketing is all about. Marketing is mandatory as you set up your home-based business, important as a long-term strategy, and absolutely necessary to ensure continued success. Your goal every day should be to find new markets for your products and services. As a beginner, appreciating the importance of constant promotion and continuous marketing is your first step in attracting customers and building an image. Fortunately, marketing your company doesn't have to be expensive or difficult. It only takes planning, creativity, and resourcefulness, talents you already have.

Remember that you're what makes your catering company different from every other catering company. In the final analysis you're not only selling parties, you're selling yourself. You're the most effective marketing tool your company has. Start thinking of how to sell yourself even before you open your business. What do you plan to do that's different, unusual, or essential? What knowledge, ideas, or contacts do you have that will help you sell yourself and your company? If you will spend the time it takes to learn and track effective marketing techniques, you'll find that your ideas, suggestions, and creativity turn into business.

Your next step is talking to the people closest to you to generate some good old-fashioned word-of-mouth advertising. Ask your church group if they have a designated caterer for celebrations after christenings. Might your temple have a referral list of caterers for planning a bat or bar mitzvah? What about your husband's law office—who coordinates the parties to entertain clients or find new associates? How about groundbreaking or new-building parties from the general contractor who lives next door? What about client leads from your real estate agent for housewarmings? Or would he or she like to buy gift baskets of your pasta sauces for his or her new clients?

I first started teaching cooking classes to attract clients to my home-based catering business. I wrote and taught classes such as "Perfect Party Recipes for the Holidays" and "Easy Turkey Dinner and Trimmings for a Crowd." By reading a local newspaper, I discovered that the local food editor ran a free column about cooking classes each Thursday in the food section. I constantly sent her information about upcoming classes. My credits read, "Denise Vivaldo, chef and partner of Martin-Vivaldo Party Planners." Not only did the listings produce business, but many of my students became clients.

Check the society page of your local newspaper every week and start to get involved in community activities. The more people you know, the more people who will get to know you and the services you can provide.

Sell, Sell, Sell

I had a strong background in sales when I opened my home-based catering business. During the years I spent working in a real estate firm, I went to seminars on sales techniques, classes on public speaking, and training programs for those who want to hone their competitive edge. I learned to make offers, sell, and negotiate. I needed these same skills to open my own business. When you're a caterer the client "offers" you the chance to handle his or her party, you "sell" your version to the client, and the two of you then negotiate.

I do think that caterers have an advantage over realtors when it comes to sales: Everyone loves to talk about food. *An example:* Cold calls. People are instantly interested in talking about throwing a party, even with a stranger; but they're not always comfortable with a discussion about selling their home. It's also easier to "upsell" clients in catering—in other words to get them to spend more money and think in grander terms.

Of course not everyone switches into catering from sales, but whatever your background, know that the ability to sell your food, your ideas, and your services is an absolute necessity in this business. If you have never made a cold call or bid and closed a deal or walked up to a stranger and offered to sell your services, consider taking a course on developing your sales technique.

Set specific goals for yourself to help develop your skills: one cold call every day, at least three introductions to new people every week, five promotional packages to good leads with cover letters each month. Fortunately you'll find that loving what you do makes selling your services much easier. This chapter is designed to help you, too, by supplying you with marketing tips and techniques. Simply choose those that feel the most natural to you.

And remember this cardinal rule in sales: Never take no for an answer; just rephrase the question.

Defining Your Niche

To define your niche you need to know your area's demographics, research the competition, and decide what kinds of clients (and catering) appeal to you.

You gathered a lot of this information when you wrote the market analysis portion of your business plan. Studying it will help you market your business successfully and target the clients you want to reach.

To get a fix on what your prospects are, you'll need to size up the different types of catering going on in your marketplace. Is there a lot of catering or only seasonal work? Are the other caterers in your town busy or strictly part-time? What clients do you think you'd be most suited to? Do you imagine yourself preparing elegant dinner parties on the weekends or delivering box lunches to offices five days a week?

These days, catering can be divided into three categories: social, corporate, and community affairs. The needs of the client differ in each case.

Social Catering

Here we're talking about weddings, anniversaries, bat or bar mitzvahs, sweet-sixteen parties, and other occasions that people plan to celebrate once in a lifetime. I call these the emotional, "hand-holding" events of life. Families may have set aside money to pay for these occasions for years, and whether the economy is weak, strong, or indifferent, traditions like these are likely to go on.

When it comes to celebrating milestone events, caterers are entrusted with more than the food: They're expected to provide memories as well—no small task. In many instances the client may never have used a caterer before (now you know where the hand-holding comes in).

If social catering is a niche that interests you, create channels to get your name around. Find out which churches or rental halls are booked for weddings or receptions in your town and leave cards and menu packages with the managers. Contact every baker that makes wedding cakes and see if you can develop a referral system. Introduce yourself at bridal-wear and rental shops. Many times the bride shops for her dress first, before the caterer, and a reference from the shop owner can be an introduction for you.

Corporate Catering

Daily breakfast meetings, snack baskets, or lunch boxes are viewed as time-management techniques in today's business world—they cut down on the time people spend out of the office. Caterers are often called on to deliver food to offices for executives' use or for management-training seminars. And nearly every corporation throws an annual holiday party where a caterer's services may be desired.

Corporate catering is much less personal than social catering. Most of the time in-house company party planners have budget guidelines and limited time to spend on setting up the catering. They are shopping for price and convenience. You may not meet the corporate party planner you're working with until the day of the event. His or her decisions will be made based on your brochure or menu package. The transaction can be handled through the mail, over the phone, or by fax. Arranging these caterings takes less of your time.

If you know the business world already, the corporate niche might appeal to you. Target corporations by calling their head offices and asking for the name of the person who handles their special events or meetings. With the correct contact name, you have the opportunity to direct information about you and your business to the people with decision-making power.

Community Affairs

The third catering market is community affairs. This includes catering local fund-raisers, charity auctions, or perhaps a town's library opening. I charge these customers the same as private clients because my costs are the same. Occasionally, however, I'll donate a gift or service in order to gain some free publicity.

For example, once I contacted the local American Heart Association regarding its annual February bake sale and volunteered to work on the coordinating committee. I was appointed chairperson. I contacted fifteen bakeries and five caterers, all of whom were willing to sell their product at cost to the committee and donate time to the fund-raiser. My idea for the theme was "Our Town's Generous Sweetheart Table." All my costs for decor were approved for reimbursement, and I donated my time. I designed platter-sized red hearts for all the baked goods and garlands of white doilies to dress up the tables. When the cookies and cakes arrived, we marked up the goods for sale, waited on the customers, and made a considerable profit for the Heart Association. Along with the other caterers and bakeries, I received publicity in the local newspapers and on radio spots, and our names appeared on big banners all around town.

As a home-based caterer, you have more flexibility than a caterer whose overhead is high, which means you can move into the market you're most comfortable with first. Most caterers work in all three niches. It keeps their businesses well-rounded financially and covers all leads to client exposure.

Choosing a Name and Logo

The name of your company may be the first words potential clients ever hear about you. For this reason your company name should be memorable and should indicate the services you provide. I think it's helpful if it reflects your personality as well.

Choosing a name is a big step that requires careful consideration. Here are a few pointers to keep in mind:

- Make the name simple to pronounce and easy to spell. If it's long or complicated, people won't repeat it out of fear of sounding foolish.
- Look in your phone book to see what your competition is named. How do you respond to those names? Do they make sense? Which names stand out from the crowd?
- Compile a list with the competitions' names and twenty potential names for your company and ask your family, friends, purveyors—anyone you can engage in conversation—which names they like and why. Call these same people back three days later and ask what names they remember.

- Be careful not to pick a name too similar to that of another company in town. If you do, you'll end up with a lot of wrong numbers, lost mail, and confused orders.
- Consider using your own name as part of your company name: Alison Stone's Corporate Catering, for example. If you do, you may not have to file a fictitious-business-name statement with your locality.
- So-called "fictitious" or "assumed" business names—in other words, names without your own name in them, such as Party Planners or Devilish Desserts—should be registered. Call your local chamber of commerce or county courthouse for more information on registering your business's name. Most localities have a list of all fictitious business names registered in the area so that you can check to make sure that you're the only person using a particular name.

Many people think that filing a fictitious-name statement will protect their use of a trade or fictitious name. It will not. Generally, filing a fictitious-business statement in most localities will only allow you to open a bank account under that name.

To properly protect a trade name, a trade search must be done, which includes a search of business directories, phone books, and rosters of professional organizations. Companies exist that will conduct name searches, but your best bet is to go to a lawyer who specializes in "intellectual property" law. As competition has increased, this has become an increasingly complicated area of the law.

It's not absolutely necessary that you have a logo, but it helps to establish a professional image. If you can't design one yourself, ask a friend with a MacIntosh computer or a design student from a local art school to give you four or five choices.

Another option is to use one of the logos available from printers who do business cards; or check out independent shops with in-house graphic designers, many of whom will work with you on a logo at reasonable rates. Remember that a successful logo needs to accentuate your style and your name; it also needs to grab people's attention.

Take the time to choose your company name and logo wisely. It's the first step in building your reputation.

Designing Promotional Pieces

Your business card is your first promotional piece. When we were just starting out, my partner found a great printer who suggested that we print on both sides of our business cards. It was a terrific idea. We used the back of the card to describe our commitment to fine foods and perfect service in a single paragraph. Clients ended up quoting to their friends from the paragraph. (We, in turn, sent a lot of clients to this smart printer.)

Once your cards are printed up, think about your second promotional piece. Proven most successful: matchbooks. (Women who don't even smoke will keep them in their purses forever.) Look in the Yellow Pages for companies listed under "merchandising." Call and ask for their catalogs, which contain thousands of inexpensive novelties you can buy imprinted with your name.

Never go anywhere without lots of cards and matches. Hand them out two at a time: one to keep and one to give away. Remember that everyone you meet—and certainly every guest at every party you cater—is a potential client. Have plenty of matchbooks around for them.

You can make additional contacts by giving away an inexpensive promotional item, such as a refrigerator magnet with your logo and phone number on it. Ask the manager of your favorite retail appliance store if you can stand out in front one afternoon with a basket of magnets and pass them out to foot traffic. Better yet, ask the store manager if you can set up a card table with cookies, lemonade, and a guest book.

Your goal is to get your name out to the public. I never leave a restaurant without leaving a 30 percent tip and two business cards underneath it. Good waiters are trained to sell, and often they come into contact with one hundred people in a shift. Make your services known to everyone: the most successful members of your chamber of commerce, the president of your homeowner's association, the mayor's secretary, the director of your town auditorium or convention center, and the general manager of your local news station. One of the best ways to do this is to buy a listing in the Yellow Pages. When people look for caterers, they often begin with the phone book. Remember that the listings are in alphabetical order, so make sure that the name of your business doesn't relegate you to the end of the list.

A Yellow Pages ad should include the following information:
- business name and phone number prominently displayed
- address
- a brief description of what your business offers
- motto or trademark services statement
- logo, if space permits
- specialty, if you have one
- length of time in business, if appropriate

Here is a sample Yellow Pages Ad:

ASTRO FOODWORKS AND DESIGN
catering services since 1984

Our creative menus and elegant set-up and design
will make your next

WEDDING	COCKTAIL PARTY
SPECIAL OCCASION	GRAND OPENING
DINNER PARTY	and more . . .

a memorable experience.

1234 City Avenue
Los Angeles, CA
555-1234

When you select purveyors, give them eye-catching sweat-shirts or hats with your logo to wear around town. Replace them when they look faded. Call your local sign shop and find out what it would cost to get your name and logo replicated on a plastic decal or magnetic panel for your car doors or van side panels. Think marketing wherever you are. You'll come up with plenty of new ways to get your name around.

As your business grows, you can take your company philosophy, style, and success and broadcast it with a brochure. A brochure doesn't have to be expensive—it just has to be attention getting. To keep costs down you can use a single 8.5 x 11 piece of colored paper folded it into thirds so that it fits inside a business envelope. Design each section separately. You might give your company's name, address, phone number, and logo on the front, a short description of the company inside, and some quotes from satisfied customers on the back. Write and design every marketing or promotion piece so that it's easy to read and understand. You can keep costs down by hiring local graphic design students or by composing it yourself on a computer. If you're feeling inspired, you might even make one-of-a-kind brochures using construction paper, pressed herbs, and calligraphy. Every time you mail out a brochure or any other promotional piece, make sure that you follow up with a phone call. There's no better way to make a good impression.

Make Your Menus Part of Your Marketing Program

Your passion for food and your skill for entertaining are the natural resources you bring to your business. One of the best ways to broadcast your passion and skill in what you do is to use your menus as marketing tools. Design your menus to showcase your style, talent, and knowledge. If your clients could cook like you, they wouldn't need to hire you. Make sure that you show them you're an expert.

Menus can function as information packets or as great direct mailers. My partner and I once booked fifteen parties in a matter of days by using our menus as the centerpiece of a direct-mail campaign. We had a target to hit when we designed the piece; we wanted to sell parties of a hundred people, strictly buffet, for Sunday afternoons over the next eleven months of the new year. We sent the piece out on January 12 (for the first week of the month, people are still recuperating from last year's parties). We used our existing client list and also addressed 400 envelopes to families in our neighborhoods.

We divided an 8.5 x 11 piece of paper on the computer into four boxes, each highlighting a different season's menu priced from $18 to $32 for complete dinners based on one hundred guests. The format encouraged clients to think about having a party any time of year.

On the reverse side of the paper, we printed tips for the hostess: Have one big party this year to pay back everyone you owe; invite people over you never get to see away from work; ask every neighbor you don't know, make it a big block party. We explained why having the party on Sunday afternoon was nicer for guests with children and how it enabled them to make it a family day. We also said it was nice for single people to have something to do on Sunday, not just Saturday night. We told the hostess that our menu had been priced to reflect the fact that Sunday isn't as busy a catering day as Saturday. To keep costs down even more, we suggested using disposable plates for appetizers and desserts. We even gave them a suggested bar list with the approximate dollar amount we thought they would spend at the liquor store. We also advised them not to clean until the day after the party. Once one hundred people arrive, who can tell if the floors are spotless or not?

We enclosed a stamped postcard asking them two simple questions: Would you like us to call about booking a party? If so, would you prefer paying all at once or in three or four easy payments?

We didn't spend money on typesetting. Instead we used a special font on the computer. We printed 500 menus at a speedy press and stuffed each one in an envelope with two business

Sample Four Seasons Menu

Spring

Fennel sprinkled Parmesan sticks
Poached salmon with fresh dill mayonnaise
Green beans and mushrooms sautéed in herbed butter
Endive and radicchio salad
Strawberry-rhubarb pie

Summer

Cold purée of spinach soup with crostini
Veal scallops dressed with lemon and parsley
Glazed carrot rounds
Garden salad with Balsamic vinaigrette
Pears and cherries in custard tarts

Fall

Mixed antipasto
Osso buco braised in wine
Roasted new potatoes
Escarole salad with red onion and black olives
Charlotte aux Poires

Winter

Crudité platter with warm artichoke dip
Sausage stuffed trout
Tri-colored roasted peppers
Roasted red potatoes with rosemary
Chocolate mousse with zest of orange

cards. We received thirty-four phone calls and booked fifteen parties. It cost us six hours of our time, $200 in stationery supplies, $145 in stamps, and $35 in business cards.

Of course we reaped plenty of referrals from that one mailing, and one party led to another. We even received one phone call from a woman saying she got our number from the employee bulletin board at work and could she buy baskets of cookies for Christmas.

Make your menus part of a long-term marketing strategy. Send out new menus—quarterly or seasonally or whatever you budget for—and keep doing it. Even if you don't get feedback right away, people enjoy the chance to stay informed.

Standing Out from the Crowd

It isn't enough simply to come up with a snazzy name, logo, and brochure (though it surely helps). You also need to distinguish yourself from other caterers in your area. Let me tell you what worked for me when I opened my home-based catering business.

After I had catered a half-dozen parties, I called clients, guests, purveyors, and staff workers and asked them all the same question: What, if anything, made my parties distinctive? They all said the same thing, as if they had been reading from a script. The food was great, but the presentation was spectacular. With that I had my hook. From that point forward I made sure that every buffet table, every flower arrangement, and every appetizer tray my guests saw looked spectacular.

Show-stopping displays became my trademark. Early on in my career, I worked with a couple who wanted to get married in a week. The bride wanted to serve nothing but seafood, caviar, and champagne. She had already called two other caterers who said it couldn't be done on such short notice and who hated the menu besides. I not only told the bride I could do the job in seven days but also came up with a wonderful way to present her menu.

With such a limited menu, I felt that the food served at the reception had better be the finest in the world. With the bride and groom's blessing, I bought the biggest shrimp (eight to a pound) from Louisiana, the finest Maine lobster tails, and the most succulent Alaskan king crab claws. I ordered an exquisite mermaid ice sculpture in whose outstretched hands I placed an enormous tin of Iranian beluga caviar. Using cookie cutters, I turned toast points for the caviar into shells, sea horses, and fish. Sprays of white orchids and a blue light box underneath the ice sculpture completed the buffet. A couple of waiters in black tuxedos served French champagne. The display was a knockout, and my labor costs were agreeably low.

This presentation of rare seafood and champagne made the guests feel as if they were attending a once-in-a-lifetime party, just the feeling the bride wanted to convey. The wedding worked so well that I booked three parties from it.

In your search for your hook, study the marketplace ads, menus, fliers, and brochures sent out by the competition. What are they doing to make themselves stand out from the crowd? Are you impressed or not? If you are, call and compliment the caterer on his or her brochure or business logo and ask who came up with such a clever idea. Also ask whether the piece created more business. Remember: The whole point of any marketing you do is to increase the growth of your business.

Keeping a Portfolio

Don't forget to take pictures of every event you cater and every product you produce. (If you can't take the pictures yourself, you can keep costs down by hiring students from a photography school.) Show these to clients the next time you're trying to sell yourself and your services. In time you'll be in a position to expand your portfolio with videos, letters of recommendations, and awards. My own portfolio is bursting with pictures of celebrities I've catered for, newspaper clippings covering the events with descriptions of my menus, and even a film clip from a Thanksgiving scene where I appeared as the caterer on a highly rated television show.

Ideas to Help You Sell Yourself as a Pro

The Professional's Approach	The Amateur's Approach
Be firm with client when necessary; stick to the terms of your proposal and budget	Try to accommodate the client's every wish (the "customer is always right" syndrome)
Come up with creative solutions to problems	Say "It can't be done"
Document the party from proposal to checklists to employee records to follow-up notes	Rely on your memory to organize the party, as well as answer questions that may arise months after the party
Take pride in your industry	Speak disparagingly of your competition
Make sure you stand out from the crowd; promote your talents	Rely on word of mouth to boost your business
Fess up to your mistakes	Blame anyone else—even the client!—for snafus
Plan every detail ahead of time	Deal with things as they arise
Send thank yous to clients, purveyors, suppliers, etc.	Never say thank you

An effective portfolio can be worth hundreds of dollars in additional sales. Once I was working with a British event planner representing a Swedish manufacturer who was planning a reception for a Japanese dignitary. They all wanted a traditional American barbecue. I submitted one barbecue menu with three different presentations: One party used paper plates and checkered tablecloths, the second party relied on a swimming pool location and Hawaiian shirts, the third was a Wild West Hoedown. It was no contest all because I had fabulous pictures of a Western Hoedown I had staged the year before. After seeing the pictures of covered wagons, hay bales, waiters as gunfighters, waitresses as saloon girls (and me dressed as Miss Kitty from the television show *Gunsmoke*), the client was more than willing to increase the cost of the party for the additional decor.

Your portfolio offers proof that you can deliver your ideas and creativity.

Putting Together a Promotional Kit

Promotional kits are handy for two reasons: They can help you land new clients, and you can use them as press kits to gain free publicity for your company from food editors, magazines, and radio shows.

My promotional kit consists of a résumé, a biography, a client list, press clips on my parties, articles written about me, copies of food shots I've styled for magazines, and menus I've created—all packaged inside a bright-red oversized envelope that matches the color of my logo. Often I send a picture of myself so that clients can start feeling comfortable with me before we even meet. The whole package is designed to put a prospective client at ease by showing that I know every aspect of the business and can solve any problems that crop up because I've done it all before.

I've used the same promotional kit to send to various radio stations, suggesting that they interview me. Twice program managers have called, and I've been able to plug special events I was coordinating for civic groups.

The same press kit has gotten me a number of gigs on several cable-television food shows. Recently I began sending my press kit to people who produce infomercials. I started after I got a call from a public relations firm representing a new bread machine. The firm had heard of me from the local cooks' bookstore. They were looking for a chef to complement their celebrity cook, who didn't know how to make bread. The idea was to show my hands in close-up shots. I didn't get the job, but the experience made me aware of a whole new market.

As you put together a promotional kit to help you launch your business, consider what you want the public to know about you. Is it that you were a designer before you became a caterer and you can't help but bring that attention to detail with you? Or should you tell them that you are the great-granddaughter of the original baker in your town? Or perhaps that you collect antique copper molds and cooking utensils and often use them in your food displays? Create a package promoting your talents. You may not have much of a track record yet, but you can still offer new ideas and beautiful menus. If you can draw, create renderings of parties you hope to stage or dishes you hope to prepare. Add a few paragraphs about who you are and what you like to do. Include a recent picture. Be sure to mention any community service awards you've received and any volunteer work in which you might be involved. You don't have to reinvent the wheel; just grease the one you have.

By adding a press release, you can use this same kit to approach local food editors and managers of radio food programs. You can make their jobs easier by supplying a list of questions to ask you or a well-written interview that you are glad to let them print.

Writing articles yourself is an excellent way to get free publicity. And the higher your profile, the more opportunities will come your way. When I wrote and published an article titled "How My Expensive Culinary Degree Has Paid for Itself" in a trade paper, the dean of a local university asked me to sit on the advisory council for their hospitality/foodservice program. I accepted the position, which gives me great statewide exposure by means of the press releases they send out.

How to Write a Press Release for Pickup

The press release, when written correctly, is a quick and effective means of communicating information and an indispensable tool for overworked people of the media. A sloppy, badly written press release is counterproductive and costly—and it usually winds up in the trash.

What makes a press release work? Try the following format and write a press release that is sure to receive wide pickup.

1. In bold capital letters list contact and phone number for press release. CONTACT: JILL SANDIN (818) 506–5106.

2. Write a catchy but straightforward headline. It should spell out exactly what the reader can expect. Sometimes a good headline will inspire a story. If the headline is too long or confusing, the reader will put the press release down before he or she gets to the first paragraph.

3. List city and release date before the first sentence.

4. Don't editorialize. Keep in mind that any portion of a press release may be repeated verbatim. The tone of a press release should reflect the tone of its audience.

5. Avoid million-dollar adjectives and adverbs. Flowery prose is not an asset when writing a press release. It detracts from the purpose.

6. Include a pertinent quotation. If the press release is about someone, the quotation should be from that person or a reliable associate. If a press release is an announcement, the quotation should be from someone intimately involved (an expert) with whatever is being announced. A quotation lends credibility to a press release and very often is picked up by the press.

7. Give a closing point of reference (phone number, address, date, deadline, etc.) in the last paragraph.

8. Assume the reader knows nothing about the subject of a press release. Include all pertinent information. Make it easy for the reader to glean the essential information.

9. Keep the length down to one page, double spaced. Generally, if a press release is more than one page, it's too wordy. There are exceptions, however, to this rule. For instance, a food-product press release can be up to five pages, including recipes. In all cases be sure to double space; single-spaced type strains the eyes.

10. Never stray from the objective of a press release. If the writer of a press release can't keep on track, don't expect the reader to get the point.

Drumming Up Business

As a caterer you have the ultimate marketing weapon at your disposal: the ability to stage incredible parties with wonderful food. Put your expertise to use on your own behalf. You might plan an open house in your own home, in your commercial kitchen, or in a local park. Send invitations to everyone you know: friends, any clients, the news media, or even politicians in your town. Serve spectacular desserts and coffee. If you're outside, supply tables for other merchants to place product displays or brochures and encourage networking. Place a huge calendar in the middle of your buffet table with plenty of colored markers. Invite guests to schedule their own appointments with you to discuss their catering needs in the year ahead.

It's also good to make your services available to local charities. Most charities need caterers to help plan and orchestrate food fairs and wine-tasting events. Catering a charitable event is an excellent way to have 1,000 people discover you and your business in a single evening.

It also pays to become recognized as a food expert in your field. Volunteer to be a speaker for clubs and schools. Prepare talks such as "Global Influences on Our Food Supply" for the environmentalists in town, "Cheap Eats in Your Neighborhood" for the singles looking for meeting places, or "Healthy Foods from Around the World" for local travel agents. You never know when one of these speaking engagements will land you a paying job. For example, as an officer of the California Culinary Alumni Board, I often speak at the CCA's career recruitment days. One year a representative of a nationwide department store heard me and called me up the next day to offer me a job as a consultant coordinating celebrity-chef demonstrations throughout southern California.

The point is to give of yourself, enjoy, and get your name out there.

Getting Referrals and Repeat Business

Referrals and repeat business are the name of the game in catering. When a satisfied client presells you to a colleague or a friend or calls you up to cater another party, you save time, money and resources. Referral and repeat business are proof positive that you're building a reputation.

One of the best ways I know to get referrals and repeat business is to stay in touch with former clients. A good way is to write your own newsletter. A personal computer and $89 worth of software are all you need to produce a professional-looking document. Write a few paragraphs about an event you've just catered, together with a recipe column and news on food trends. If you're feeling ambitious, you can always include reprints of articles (be sure to get permission from the original publisher). Mail this newsletter to your client list as well as to local corporations, PTA groups, weight-control clinics, and doctors' offices in the area you want to target.

If a newsletter isn't the jam on your peanut butter sandwich, plan to send out a new menu postcard each month, or a recent party photograph, or a food treat to old clients and to anyone you'd like to have as a new client. Or just pick up the phone and say hello.

If you need to light a fire under old clients to help you find new clients, consider offering them a referral fee: 5 or 10 percent of the net profit from any party you book as a result of their leads.

Ten Ways *Not* to Get Referrals or Repeat Business

1. Assuming your clients will give out your name for referrals without your asking them.

2. Taking satisfied clients for granted and assuming they'll never find another caterer.

3. Forgetting to write a thank-you note for a referral or favor a client did for you.

4. Not complimenting a client for solving a problem for you.

5. Making a client wait for an answer.

6. Not apologizing for a mistake you made.

7. Forgetting who is paying you.

8. Taking yourself too seriously. You are not a rocket scientist; you are a caterer.

9. Hiring staff and thinking you can teach them to be polite to your clients. Hire polite and considerate people to start with.

10. Thinking that problems are never your fault but always the client's fault.

Advertising

When it comes to establishing your home-based catering business, I recommend that you get as much free publicity as you can before you think of running any ads other than a listing in the Yellow Pages.

An ad in the Yellow Pages is probably the best ad you can buy. Other types of advertising you might consider are radio spots (can be highly effective), sponsoring a Little League team (maximum goodwill), billboards (not as expensive as you think), ads in neighborhood newsletters (big bang, little bucks), or city magazines (big bucks, questionable bang).

My two problems with advertising are these: How do I know I will reach the market I want, and why is it so expensive? I've had only moderate success when paying for advertising. An ad costs me $350 to $500 in my local paper, and if I book only one party, that's not good return on my money. For $500 I can host a soiree at a swanky hotel suite, invite twenty VIPs, serve them superb Cabernet with my warm pesto Brie for an hour and walk away with thirty to forty qualified leads for clients.

I suggest you inform yourself about advertising by research, study, and interactions with professionals in the field. You can call up sale representatives from your local newspapers, magazines, and radio stations and have them show you the sales growth they track on successful accounts. Ask for a list of their satisfied clients. Or get in touch with professionals in your area who handle public relations and advertising. Ask them for a complimentary proposal of the services they would provide for you or the ads and placement they think you need. If you decide to go ahead, be sure to negotiate a campaign that you can afford.

To keep costs down maybe you can trade a service or share expenses with other accounts they handle. Or how about collaborating with a rental company or the local wedding chapel for a spring ad?

However you decide to do it, advertising will keep your name in front of the public. Your goal is to have people know that your company is living, breathing, and ready to do business.

Tracking Your Success

As you generate new business, ask clients how they found you. Was it the magnets? The open house? The newsletter? The ad you ran in the hospice magazine? The speech you gave on Career Day at your son's school? The story the food editor printed about you in the local food pages? Keep track of your promotional ideas and stick with those that pay off. Before long you'll have the pleasure of seeing your business grow by leaps and bounds.

Inexpensive pamphlets from the Small Business Directory

(Call the Office of Business Development, SBA Publications, at 800–827–5722 for ordering information.)

Creative Selling: The Competitive Edge   Explains how to use creative selling techniques to increase profits.

Marketing for a Small Business: An Overview   Provides an overview of marketing concepts and contains an extensive bibliography of sources covering the subject of marketing.

Marketing Checklist for Small Retailers   A checklist of important questions covering the areas of customer analysis, buying, pricing, promotion, and other factors in retail marketing.

Researching Your Market   Learn inexpensive techniques that you can apply to gather facts about your customer base and how to expand it.

Selling by Mail Order   Provides basic information on how to run a successful mail-order business, including information on product selection, pricing, testing, and writing effective advertisements.

Advertising   Learn how to effectively advertise your product and services.

7

Crunching the Numbers
Keeping Your Books and Paying Taxes

When you're putting together your first event, it may seem easier to gather together your receipts, pay as many expenses as you can by personal check, and figure out the rest the morning after. This is not a good idea because it may tempt you to leave everything for later. Before you know it, you won't be able to take a step without treading on bills and invoices, and what is worse, you won't know the economic health of your business in any objective way.

Instead of letting things pile up or running your business by the seat of your pants, I recommend that you make an appointment with a good accountant. Read this chapter to acquaint yourself with your options and then work with your accountant to arrive at a bookkeeping system that will help you manage your business, which is the whole point of a bookkeeping system. Not only does it help you operate your business in a professional manner, it also allows you to keep track of your income and expenses in such a way that you can analyze where your business is going. Is it hard to do? Absolutely not, so long as you do it every day.

One of my friends spent her first year in business without using any particular system. She paid her purveyors' bills as soon as she received them (never thinking she might negotiate more favorable payment terms and thus hold on to her money longer), extended credit to her clients (a terrible idea, and one designed to put you out of business), and never had enough information on hand to anticipate cash flow. Then at the end of the year, she invested in a computer bookkeeping program. "It's changed my life," she said to me. "I had no idea how much money I was spending on anything. For example, I spent way too much on new equipment, considering my income. [Your accountant will tell you that you can only deduct a maximum of $10,000 for equipment purchases, without amortization, as a direct expense, so it really doesn't make sense to purchase, as opposed to lease, more.] I also paid top dollar for a lot of the food I bought. Had I realized how much produce I was buying from one particular purveyor, I might have thought to negotiate a better price." The new bookkeeping program she's been working with keeps her business in the black and gives her access to an incredible amount of useful information.

Making Good Use of Your Accountant

Unless you are already an accounting whiz, I suggest that you sit down with your accountant as soon as possible to discuss the following five issues:

Record keeping. As a caterer, you will need to keep track of your equipment (some inevitably gets lost, broken, or abused), your inventory of food stock (if you do have a kitchen and keep stock on hand), your labor, your consumables (paper, streamers, decorations, and other disposables), your dishware, your rentals of both equipment and locations, and so on. This chapter discusses a variety of ways to keep track of all these important bits of information, from manual bookkeeping to bookkeeping by computer. Your accountant, who should know the scope of your business as well as you yourself do, is in an excellent position to advise you on which system will work best for you.

Establishing a chart of accounts.   To keep accurate books you must have a consistent set of categories to put individual items of income and expense into. This set of categories is called a chart of accounts, and it should accurately reflect your day-to-day business activities as closely as possible. Moreover, you should set it up well before you pay your first dollar to launch your new business.

First, set up a checking account to be used only for your catering business. Next, consult your accountant for help in setting up a chart of accounts. You'll find a sample basic chart of accounts in the sidebar on pages 126–27. As you can see, there are separate categories under food costs for staples, poultry, fish, and so on. This level of detail allows you to track your various costs as part of an overall effort to determine which items are the most profitable. Unless the items are broken down into meaningful categories, you won't have the information you need to analyze your expenditures, or to cut better deals with vendors.

Say after six months in business you notice that people are buying much more fish from you than chicken or meat. The trend is easy to see because "fish" is a separate item in your chart of accounts. Armed with this information, you can say to your fish vendor, "Hey, I've spent $500 [or $1,000 or $5,000] with you over the past six months. That's quite a bit of money. How about cutting me a discount any month I spend more than $100 [or $200 or $1,000]?" Without this information you'll be at a disadvantage. In fact you may lose parties to other caterers in your market area who have been able to cut better deals with purveyors based on their analysis of their own chart of accounts.

Understanding the difference between cash basis and accrual basis accounting.   Until several years ago it was popular, and legal, for many businesses to use a type of accounting called accrual basis. This method accounts for income and expenses *not*

Sample Basic Chart of Accounts

	January	February	March	1st Quarter Totals
Income				
Prop rental income	____	____	____	____
Food income	____	____	____	____
Entertainment income	____	____	____	____
Design income	____	____	____	____
Consulting income	____	____	____	____
Total Income				
Expenses				
Auto expense	____	____	____	____
Books	____	____	____	____
Cleaning	____	____	____	____
Uniform rental	____	____	____	____
Rental of kitchen	____	____	____	____
Rental of event location	____	____	____	____
Permits	____	____	____	____
Equipment lease	____	____	____	____
Telephone	____	____	____	____
Utilities	____	____	____	____
Kitchen salaries	____	____	____	____

Office salaries				
Taxes				
Insurance				
Advertising				
Entertainment				
Food costs				
Fish				
Meat				
Poultry				
Produce				
Staples				
Other				
Prepared food costs				
Desserts				
Appetizers				
Juices, mineral water,				
soft drinks				
Other beverages				
Total Expenses				
Net Profit (Loss)				

as they are paid for or received, but as against the job or party to which they are allocated. For example, let's say that you had a party in January of 1994 and were paid a deposit in December of 1993. That income would not, under the accrual basis method, be legally "received" by you until after the party in January 1994. Likewise, the monies you pay, either in December 1993 or January 1994, which are directly attributable to that party would not be "received" or "spent" according to your books until after the party in January 1994. Obviously this was a popular way for many small businesses to not pay taxes on money they received until the following tax year, so in 1987 the U.S. Congress closed the loophole for most people who were using it, such as small businesses. Most small businesses, even small corporations, must now be on cash-basis accounting and most must, unless there are extremely good reasons that your accountant will use to convince the IRS, be on a calendar-year basis. This means that unless your accountant devises some way for you to avoid it, you will have to declare income when you receive it and also deduct expenses when you pay them, and your "tax year" for your business will have to be the same as your "personal" tax year: January 1 through December 31. It is still important, however, to understand the concept of accrual-basis accounting for your budgeting purposes.

For example, let's say you have that big party on January 14, 1994, and you know that you will have to buy a lot of food and pay for a lot of expense a few days before the party; yet you've received a big deposit on December 3, 1993, and you know that you'll be taxed on that even though most of it really won't be your net income—it will go for event expenses. What do you do? Probably it would be a good idea to take as much of that money as possible and prepay as many of the event items as possible. Often your location fee will be refundable, except for a small nonrefundable deposit if you cancel within ten days, so if you prepay the location expense in December, you have shifted out much of the deposit that you received, and if your event is canceled or postponed more than ten days before January 14, you can still get your money back from the location, and you did not have to bear the tax expense on your deposit, either. These are techniques that a good accountant will teach you, and the more experienced you become, the less often you will have to call him or her to ask how to handle a particular thorny situation.

Understanding the difference between gross and net profit. Generally your gross profit on an event is what you make on an event after paying the expenses allocated specifically only to that event. So it is obvious that if you get paid $10,000 for an event and it costs $2,000 for a location, $2,000 for food, $1,000 for labor, and $1,000 for other supplies that went into that event (for a total of $6,000), you have made $4,000—or have you? What about your car, your equipment rental, and your other overhead? When you deduct these later costs, you get to "net before tax profit." Then you still have a myriad of taxes to pay before you get to the money you keep to live on.

For you to stay in business, it is absolutely essential that you know the amount of your overhead, and if you are just starting, you must be able to project the amount of what your overhead will be; otherwise, you will not end up with anything at the end of the year. Overhead items include the expenses that you pay to stay in business that cannot be assigned to one specific event. Examples of these are rent, equipment lease payments, labor costs that are not hourly such as secretarial support, professional fees such as accountants and lawyers, insurance, the cost of the use of your vehicles, and the amount of any purchased equipment such as computers, kitchen equipment, and so on. It is important that you make sure that there is enough "gross profit" to cover a pro-rata share of your overhead. This "pro-rata" share of overhead that is assigned to each event is often what people tend to forget to include in figuring out what they need to charge to break even. These expenses are just as real as the costs of food, waiters, and location. Your accountant will assist you in determining this figure, but there are two basic ways to approach it. One, probably the one you will start with, is on a calendar basis: You add up all of your overhead for the year (including your estimated taxes and an estimate of what you need to pull out of the business to live on), divide the total by 12, and the result is a monthly amount of money attributable to overhead. If you have 2 parties in one month, you add to each event's out-of-pocket expenses one-half of your monthly overhead. If you have 6 events in one month (lucky you), you need only to be sure that you add one-sixth of one month's overhead to break even. A different method is a dollar percentage. You and your accountant add to each dollar of direct-event expense a markup percentage that includes your margin for overhead, plus taxes, plus net profit (the amount you intend to pull out of the business). This is harder to arrive at, but standard industry markup figures do exist. The problem with both of these methods is that they assume regular future business and do not necessarily take into account your "start-up" costs.

Your accountant will be invaluable in assisting you with this very critical calculation. Remember, if you add on too much, you will not be competitive; if you add on too little, you will not have enough money to pay the actual costs of running your business. Computer programs—such as Quicken, which is discussed on page 136—can assist you on these calculations. For example, assuming that you have entered the appropriate information on your expenses, you can use Quicken to calculate your overhead expenses as a percentage of your total expenses.

Taxes. Taxes, as the old saying goes, are inevitable. When you are in business for yourself, they are also confusing. What your employer used to take care of, you must now take care of yourself. Suddenly you find yourself paying quarterly estimated taxes on your income, your own social security tax, sales taxes on your goods and services, and withholding and social security taxes on your employees' income.

Because taxes vary from locality to locality, be sure to check with your accountant to find out exactly what your responsibilities are. In the United States we generally pay on an honor system; the government expects us to keep track of our transactions, report them accurately, and then have the money on hand to pay the relevant taxes in a timely fashion. This is where a lot of small businesses get in trouble—their owners do not plan well and do not have the money on hand to pay their taxes when due. The government can, and often does, assess interest and penalties and

Possible Business Deductions

Accounting Fees
Advertising
Attorney's fees
Automobile use
Bad debts
Conventions and trade shows
Depreciation expenses
Dues to industry groups
Gifts
Insurance
Interest
License fees
Office supplies
Partial entertainment
Portfolio materials
Rent: Kitchen
Salaries, bonuses, and commissions

may even take your possessions. In fact you can even be thrown in jail! As a preventive measure, you must work out a plan with your accountant for paying your taxes on a timely basis.

This is an area where you can't afford to make a mistake. For example, if you have employees who require withholding (be sure to check with your accountant, as you may need to withhold money even for waiters you use only a couple of times a year) and you fail to withhold the appropriate taxes, you can quickly get in arrears and then in serious trouble. The same is true for sales tax or your own estimated taxes. If you have put in enough hard work to make a net profit and you have not pre-paid your own taxes, you could be liable for a penalty plus interest. A small business can quickly be buried by tax liabilities like these.

This book will not, and cannot, address the tax issue in more detail (except to list the types of deductions a caterer ought to keep track off—see sidebar on page 131) because taxes vary widely from location to location and the tax laws are constantly changing. Consult your trusty accountant without delay.

Accounting Systems

Several types of accounting systems are currently in use: manual systems; private, professional bookkeeping companies; computer systems; and the "I have no system until I panic at the end of the tax reporting quarter" system. For obvious reasons try to avoid the latter.

The manual system has several points in its favor. First of all it is the least expensive to acquire. Examples of this system are the "one-write" and "pegboard" type of devices that incorporate ledger cards with the checks you write. Each time you write a check, you put the appropriate ledger card under it, and a carbon copy of the check amount is made on the ledger card. You will have one ledger card for each bookkeeping account listed in your chart of accounts. For instance, when you write a check for your monthly payment for your business telephone bill, you would put the "telephone and messenger" ledger card under the check so that as you write the check, the same information is recorded on the card. If you do this faithfully, you will always have accurate, up-to-date information about what you have spent for each category in your chart of accounts. A good source for these systems is NEBS business forms, and they can be reached at their toll-free number: (800) 225–6380. Be sure to request a catalog. NEBS also has a nice assortment of invoices and other forms.

There *are* drawbacks to this system:

- You must total it manually; in other words you will not have a current total unless you manually add the items on the card each time.
- If you write one check to cover items that ought to be on

several accounting cards, you're in trouble. For example, if you write a check to a purveyor who sells you both fish and meat and you have separate accounts for fish and meat, you will have a hard time splitting the amounts.

- Because it is a manual system, it does not have anywhere near the speed and flexibility of a modern computer system, which, if money is time, is worth a fortune in savings.

Another option is to use a professional bookkeeping service. These companies come into your workplace periodically (or you drop off your check book at their offices) to input your check register into a computerized accounting system, which will then give you and your accountant the information you need in the appropriate format. These companies can also handle payroll and deposits to the appropriate taxing agencies. Another advantage of using one of these services is that you can call and speak to someone who can explain things to you, which can be reassuring when your business is in its infancy. Another plus is that you pay as you go. There is little or no initial investment and no need to learn computer programs. So if you are easily frustrated and want to leave the bookkeeping expertise to others, you can hire someone to take care of your books for you.

The disadvantages of using an outside service to do your bookkeeping are (1) you are dependent on others to give you access to the information you need about how your business is running, (2) in the long run an outside service is more expensive, (3) you will have no real incentive or opportunity to become acquainted with the ins and outs of computers and how they can make your life easier and more efficient.

I have to admit that I am in favor of modern technology, especially the personal computer. It is possible to save so much time when you use one that, in my opinion, it is a very serious error in business judgment not to use one. Some of you may have been using the excuse that you're a chef, an artist who is "too creative for such mundane things" (I know because I used this excuse myself for many years). Nevertheless, if you have been afraid to learn how to use computers or have not had the chance yet, my advice is: "Get over it, real fast!" A computerized business system allows you to generate checks and have that information automatically entered into your accounting system. You can even transfer all this information to another program that allows you to estimate your taxes. The cost savings in bookkeeping and accountants' fees are phenomenal. The only drawbacks to a computerized accounting system are (1) the initial cost of the hardware and software and (2) your "learning curve" in studying how to use the programs. If you are mechanically inclined and have any patience at all, I recommend that you spend about $1,700 for a computer system, another $50 to $200 for some accounting software, and thus enter the modern era of information access.

Buying Computers and Software

You may already know that there are two major types of consumer computer systems currently available: IBM-Compatible, also known as PCs, DOS, or MS-DOS systems, and Apple systems, also known as Mac or Macintosh. I strongly recommend using the DOS type of machines and software because (1) they are less expensive, (2) you'll have many more software programs available to you, (3) they are used more often in catering and business, (4) with accompanying Windows programs, they are as easy to use as a Mac or even easier, (5) they have a greater choice of peripherals (computer talk for printers, mice, modems, fax/modems, and such), and (6) they are more stable—in my experience, they don't get "stuck" as often as Mac-based computers. Also, and perhaps most important, there is a much greater variety of DOS computers to buy, which means that you have a better chance to get one that is tailored to your needs.

I suggest getting a notebook computer, and if it is your first computer, you might want to get one with a well-known brand name and with a well-developed support system, such as AST, Zenith, Dell, or IBM. Notebook computers are designed to be light and transportable, which means that you can take them with you from job to job, location to location, and then home again. They weigh 6 pounds or less (some weigh as little as 4 pounds) and are just as fast and can hold as much information as the larger, nonportable desktop computers. For example, you can get an entry level notebook computer, loaded with most of the software you will need, for about $1,400. Zenith makes a machine called a Z-Lite that weighs in at about 3½ pounds, and travels very well—it's about half the size of a legal pad and costs about $2,400. If you want to go to the extra expense, you can even get a notebook computer with a color screen.

You will also need a printer. I recommend Hewlett-Packard's DeskJet 500. This ink-jet printer costs about $400 to $500, prints all the letters, invoices, accounting statements, and other information you will need to print beautifully; it also is compatible with most major brands of computers and most major software programs. If you are doing fliers, promotions, invitations, etc., with your computer, or if you think you ever will, you can buy a COLOR DeskJet 500C for about $700. (That's right, it will print in color!) This gives you a tremendous edge in marketing because people respond to color much more than to black and white.

When you buy a computer, consider buying the most current version of Microsoft Windows to run with it. This is a program that runs all your other programs; it lets you select the program you want to use at the moment and can transfer information between them. It operates much the same way as a Mac: Using a mouse, you point to icons and click when you want something done. It makes things fun and intuitive.

This type of "program manager" is referred to as your "environment." When you get your other programs, such as those for word processing, they must be designed to fit your "environment."

Word-Processing Programs
For word processing I recommend that you use Microsoft Word for Windows or Ami-Pro by Lotus, which not only has a spell checker but also a grammar-checking program in it to correct your grammar and spelling in an instant. Both of these programs are rather expensive, so you might want to stick with MS Write, which is a modest word-processing program that comes with Windows 3.1 at no extra charge. It doesn't have a lot of bells and whistles, but it gets the job done.

Accounting Programs
In my opinion when it comes to keeping books by computer, Quicken (published by Intuit) wins hands down. You can buy Quicken for Windows or Quicken for DOS, depending on which environment you have selected. In either case the program will allow you to track all of your income and expenses by the categories you choose. You can keep track of your income and expenses per job as well as per time period. If you elect to use its check-writing functions, it will fill in checks that you buy specifically for your printer.

Once you're up and running, Quicken generates cash-flow reports, income statements, balance sheets, and much more. It tracks payables and receivables and can even print payroll checks. Best of all, it's user friendly. If you buy Quicken for Windows, you can get it with Quicken Invoicing, which will calculate and print custom invoices for you.

Invoicing

Some people are shy when it comes to invoicing. You can rest assured that many clients will gleefully take advantage of this. As I've said before, be sure to get at least a 50 percent deposit when you sign a contract. If your client has a hard time giving you a deposit, they will be worse when it comes time to collect the balance. I have developed a rule of thumb: *Never, ever* spend any of my own money for someone else's event; that is what the deposit money is for. (I even ask my dear, sweet mother for deposit money. I mean it.) The easiest way to get burned is by "last-minute manipulators." This is the name I give to people who tell you that they need you for a last minute rush job the day after next and they can't possibly give you a check at the time because they are out of checks, and the president of the company is on vacation, and the checks are only cut on Wednesday out of the accounting office, or some such story. You can bet dollars to doughnuts that if you ever get paid, it will be weeks or months after the event and after many angry calls by you.

Also be sure to get the entire balance owed you three days before the day of the event because this is the last time that you will have effective leverage with your client. Collecting all the money before the event is strictly good sales technique and policy. You can do this in a professional manner by letting your client know that these are the only terms you work with. You'll be happy to do the work for them, but because you will lay out a lot of time, talent, knowledge, and your reputation to make their party happen, you feel that the goodwill must flow both ways.

The Artist Versus the Businessperson: Why So Many Caterers Fail

Someone once said that the greatest thing in the world is to have the freedom to do what you love to do. Why didn't Mr. Someone just come out and say the greatest thing in the world is money? You may be great at what you do, love what you're doing, have lots of talent, new friends, and business booked, but if you are not making a profit, your company is not going to last. If you continue not to make a profit, your catering business is a hobby, and an expensive one at that.

Far too many people in catering love what they are doing but overlook the obvious fact of life that they have to support themselves—*until* ugly reality knocks at the door or comes in the mail. You need vision, drive, enthusiasm, and faith to succeed, but I suggest that you do not mislead yourself into thinking that these merits alone will sustain you. You need to be very practical and make your business work within a financial framework. Once you are on solid financial ground, you can feel secure that you have created a company that will sustain you artistically as well as financially.

Catering can be lucrative, exciting, and fun. Is there anything wrong with being a rich artist?

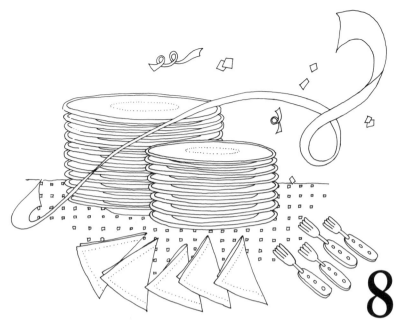

8

Setting the Stage
for a Successful Party

Before you do anything make sure you have a signed contract or proposal from your client, a minimum guest guarantee, and half the cost of the party in your hand.

Put every party on paper. Invent a system of checklists to use for every one. Checklists make your preparations disaster-proof.

Before the Party

You've worked out a theme with your client. Now get set to roll up your sleeves and make it happen.

Get estimates and references; interview subcontractors for job bids as designers, florists, entertainers, and photographers. This is what full-service catering is all about. It's standard practice to mark up all support-service fees by 10 to 20 percent and include the cost in your bill. You need this cushion to reimburse your company for time, telephone calls, expertise, and coordinating skills.

It's well worth your while to use your best sales techniques to convince your client to buy these services from you. Even if clients hire these services themselves, you still end up as coordinator. Why? Because the caterer is the party's ringmaster. All these services depend on how and at what time you serve the food.

At the very least charge a coordination fee. Clients will understand if you explain the time you must spend on their event. Don't give away time or ideas. They are something you provide for a fee, just like quality food.

You will need to have signed contracts or agreements with all the subcontractors you use, and you will have to provide them with deposit money to reserve their time. It is important to stay in touch with them through the months of preplanning. Don't assume they know what you or your client expects. Each party is different.

Two weeks before each party, I send an information sheet, "Information You Should Know before the Party," to every subcontractor. I follow through with a phone call to verify that they've received it, and I ask them to review it with me by phone. This information includes the exact location of the party and how to get there, the amount of time they are expected to put in, and the time they should arrive for setup. I add instructions about where they can park, what they should wear, and where they can change clothes if necessary. I let them know whether the client is paying for them to eat, too, or not. I remind them that drugs of any kind are illegal. I ask if they'll need a closet with a lock to secure any additional items and whether they have insurance for their equipment—and for themselves—in case the host's insurance doesn't cover them.

While I'm writing up this information, I make a separate list for myself:

1. Order an extra tablecloth for the disk jockey's card table.
2. Bring extra black duct tape to secure the photographer's cables and light cords.
3. Check to see that the buffet tables are strong enough to support the designer's props.

4. Bring cosmetic sponges and facial tissue for blotting the makeup of the costumed servers.

Mistakes happen if you don't double-check and put everything in writing. At one party, a black-tie affair, we were expecting a three-piece jazz combo, but the musicians arrived dressed in Hawaiian shirts with Congo drums! At another party, a wedding cake was delivered to the wrong restaurant, and I had to carry five tiers of spun-sugar bridges, fountains, and figurines through heavy traffic on a busy street. One time flowers arrived so late that we passed them out as good-bye gifts to departing guests.

My worst mistake was hiring a photographer who smoked in the bathroom, set off the smoke detector, and brought out the local fire department. I had to evacuate 300 guests and my entire staff five minutes before dinner was to be served and keep them out until the firemen discovered the culprit in a stall in the john.

Rule of thumb: Make it easy on yourself and others by discussing your expectations for their performance days before the event.

Organizing Your Time and the Party Setup

If you didn't have time to visit the location at the time you wrote the proposal, go now. Preview the site at the same time of day that the party will be held. Are there parking restrictions at this time? Traffic? Barking dogs? Garbage cans waiting for pickup? Are there adequate lights, safe walkways, temperature changes, or strong winds? Will you need a security guard to watch gifts or to keep out party crashers? A portable phone for emergencies? If you rent a van, is there a place to park it, with easy access to the kitchen? Where are you going to seat the guests for dinner? Is the location on different levels, and will you need a set of walkie-talkies to keep in touch with your waiter three flights up?

You can kill two birds with one stone by meeting the representative from the rental company you're working with at the same time you do the site inspection. Ask him for suggestions and help with your logistical problems. Most rental companies will draw up blueprints or layouts free of charge. They draw details of seating to scale as well as buffet arrangements or temporary kitchen facilities. No matter how small the party, get professional input before you even move a couch to make room for a single table. Rental companies are successful because of referrals and repeat customers. They'll do the little jobs in hopes of getting bigger ones.

After your site inspection, build a comprehensive rental list. If your client decides that he or she wants a dance floor or a tent in the backyard, a rental company will handle such special needs.

For one wedding I catered, the hostess ran out of room in her backyard as the guest count grew. I called a rental company, and they covered the swimming pool with wooden scaffolding and Astroturf. Another fifty guests were seated there for dinner.

Some rental companies give caterers cash commissions or discounts at the end of each month based on the amount of business the caterer brings in. Sometimes they give a referral fee for directing the client to them and allowing the rental company to deal on its own with the client. (If you do this, though, get a copy of the rental list to make sure you get everything you need.

Whether you rent or the client rents depends on what you are comfortable with. How much time do you have, and how much can you handle? The more you take on, the more careful you must be in budgeting your time and money, but the greater is your opportunity for profit.

Another option is for you to invest in some catering gear yourself. Often home-based caterers end up catering small parties or weekly service clubs like Kiwanis or Elks consistently enough that they feel it's a worthwhile investment to buy dishes and flatware. You bill the client for the use of this equipment, which pays for itself after only a few parties. The money you generate this way soon becomes a fund for the purchase of more equipment.

For example: My partner and I bought beautiful burnished-brass chafers. They were better looking than any offered by the rental companies, yet I charged my clients half the going rental rate. After only twelve parties the chafers had paid for themselves. And then I found that if I needed to sweeten the pie in a

Setup Times

Estimated Time	Type of Function (for 100 guests)
½ hour	simple cocktail party, nearby delivery door
1 hour	simple party, distant delivery door
1½ hours	simple party, distant delivery door, heavy equipment
1½ hours	buffet, nearby delivery door, medium setup, moderate equipment
2 hours	buffet, distant delivery door, medium setup, moderate equipment
2½ hours	complex cocktail reception, nearby delivery door, heavy equipment
3 hours	sit-down dinner, nearby delivery door, heavy equipment
4 hours	very complex party with multiple food-serving stations and heavy equipment

competitive bid, I let clients have them at no charge. It was cheaper than giving food or my time away, yet it provided good-will and stimulated referrals.

At your first meeting and on-site inspection, decide the time your rentals must arrive and begin to estimate how long it will take to unload, set up, and break down the party. Study the party layout and place an X on each spot where you need personnel. Can you do it alone? If not, how long do you think each job will take?

Try to anticipate the amount of time for everything by walking through the party and the menu on paper from start to finish. Will you need an extra pair of hands to unload the van because there is no elevator? What about that grill ten minutes away from the kitchen in the backyard? Where can you put the bar so that it is easy for guests to get to it the moment they arrive without blocking anything or anyone? And do you have the rental representative's phone number (or better yet, beeper number) in case you've forgotten something?

I've gone as far as taking pictures of the location, props, and sample floral pieces to be sure I know what I've discussed with a client. After the party the pictures go into my portfolio.

Moral of the story: Don't leave *any* pieces of your party to chance.

The Menu and Start-up

If your client is having trouble deciding on the menu and the party is just two weeks away, stop suggesting items and tell the client that you'll choose. Usually this makes a client decide quickly. A common mistake of new caterers is allowing clients to make last-minute decisions and changes. They cost you money, profit, and time. Clients can be just like children about testing your limits. Some of them will run you ragged if they think they can get away with it.

Prepare kitchen "prep" sheets. There are lists describing the jobs that have to be done for your menu. Distribute the jobs over several days. Do anything you can several days early (but be sure to save chores like washing the lettuce till the very end). To come up with the most complete prep sheets, pretend that you are not going to be at the party and write the prep sheets as instructions for someone else. Give this someone else as much information as you can. Start your prep lists with the appetizers and move through the courses. List everything you have contracted for down to coffee with cream and sugar or herb tea. If peanuts are to be served at the bar, write it down. It is the only way I know to guarantee you won't forget to serve anything.

Underneath each menu item on your kitchen prep sheet, make a note of special equipment you will need to bring on the day of the event and how each dish will be served. Here is a sample prep sheet:

Appetizers for 25 guests

Items: 3 types passed cold, 2 served warm (50 pieces each)
First item: 50 fluted ½-inch-tall cucumber rounds with 1 oz. piped salmon-cream mousse and lemon-fan garnish

Pack: pastry bag, star tip, zester

Serve: silver tray with pink doilies
Onion flower as tray centerpiece

Prepare at kitchen: Zest skin, slice cucumbers, whip cream cheese and smoked salmon. Slice lemons into fans. Pack all components, individually wrapped in plastic containers, in a foil pan. Cover with film wrap and label. Finish on site.

Wrapped carefully in plastic containers, this appetizer can be prepared the day before the party. By placing all the components together, you save the trouble of trying to find something in the confusion of unpacking on the site. In general pack ingredients for each course together. In this example you have designed an appetizer "kit." You could easily delegate the finishing work to someone else now. He or she has all the ingredients, equipment, and presentation instructions.

Break down every menu item this way so that your staff won't waste time looking for items that aren't there. With this method, if you have forgotten something, you'll discover it sooner—all you'll need to do is check your list.

From these prep lists you will be able to build your order sheet. Your order sheet is your shopping list. An organized order sheet should be easy to read and help keep your budget in line. I highlight product with colored pens when the orders are placed and confirmed.

At first, order sheets can be broken down into food groups, and later on, as you become more experienced, you'll probably break them down by purveyors.

A blank piece of paper divided into four squares will get you started. Write Meats/Seafoods in the first square, Produce in the second, Dry Goods and Paper Products in the third, and Dairy

Sample Order Sheet

Meats/Seafoods:
4 lbs. salmon
_____
_____
_____
_____
_____
_____

Produce:
12 cucumbers
2 iceberg lettuce
10 lemons
_____
_____
_____

**Dry Goods/
Paper Products:**
doilies
plastic containers
foil
napkins
_____
_____
_____

**Dairy/
Baked Goods:**
cream cheese
pastry shells
_____
_____
_____
_____

and Baked Goods in the fourth. List the products you need directly from your prep sheets. If you have your pantry or kitchen set up as discussed in Chapter 2, take inventory first and use as much stuff as you have on hand.

You'll make decisions about what food to make and what food to buy for every party you cater. You'll learn to balance the menu ingredients by cost, quality, time, preparation, and presentation. You'll learn to have every single menu item you can prepped or partially cooked the day before the party.

I have experimented with all kinds of food over the years looking for dishes that can be made ahead. I find that a good many, in fact, taste better made ahead than cooked at the last minute. Lasagna is a prime example of something that tastes better the second day, so cook it the day before the party and just reheat it on site. Bourbon cake also tastes better when it's been baked ahead and wrapped, resting for a week. Black bean soup with ham hocks is another dish that's best the second day when the flavors have melded and it's rich and smoky.

As your parties grow in size, you'll learn the necessity of what I call "food suspension." This is the art of storing perfectly prepped food in the refrigerator for a day or two just waiting to be finished. Experiment and test items yourself. I bet you know some already, such as marinated flank steak or chicken teriyaki skewers.

Sometimes it will be well worth your while to buy certain products already prepared. For example, when I first met my partner, she'd stay up all night baking rolls for the parties she catered. She thought because she was a caterer she had to make everything herself. After we got together I convinced her to buy the best rosemary-garlic rolls from a local bakery instead. I suggested that she could put those baking hours she saved into something else she really needed—like sleep.

I spend a lot of time looking for new products, trying samples of ready-made items, and discovering wholesale caterers' products I can buy and highlight on my menus. I am careful to pick caterers, purveyors, and manufacturers who sell only high-quality products. It's important that the food products you purchase are fresh and uncontaminated and have been handled with the utmost care to ensure their safety. Whenever something is delivered that you are doubtful about—the wrong temperature or not as fresh as you like—don't accept it, and tell that purveyor why.

With each party you cater, you'll learn more about what products you want to buy and use regularly. This will ease your work load, help you manage your time, and gradually help you perfect your menu. Better to make three dishes perfectly than five that are just average.

Along the way you'll learn to save yourself storage space and refrigeration yet guarantee freshness by having products delivered right to the party site. Ice, wine, bread, pastries, appetizers, and whole fruit can come straight to the party. This means less for you to carry to the party site and one more job you don't have to do yourself.

The luxury of a carefully planned catering menu with a correct guest count means that you know exactly what you need to buy and nothing more. I work with both new and experienced caterers every day who haven't spent enough time in preparation. Because they don't really know the scope of the event they're catering, they are scared. To compensate they make extra food, buy extra cakes, or run to the store for an extra leg of lamb "just in case"—anything to avoid running out of food. You can imagine what happens to their bottom line.

Rules to live by: Deliver what you promised, stick to your menu, guide your client to what's best for both of you, and stay within your budget.

Scheduling Staff and Assistants

As you break down party preparation into time slots, you'll discover the most efficient use of your time and wait staff. In wholesale or "drop-off" catering, where you drop off food ready for the host or hostess to serve, you can work alone.

For most social affairs, civic functions or corporate meetings, however, a caterer needs a helper or two. Remember the simple saying I tell my students: You can only be in one place at a time. So if your client has twelve guests for dinner and the hostess wants appetizers passed throughout the cocktail hours, ask yourself: Who is going to be in the kitchen getting the salads and dinner ready if I'm out on the floor passing appetizers?

After the site inspection and menu breakdown, you'll be ready to decide how much staff you'll need. If you need only one pair of hands to help, hire a person who is a jack-of-all-trades, an assistant who is well rounded and dependable. This person should be able to tend bar, wash dishes, wait, and serve.

It helps to develop a party flow sheet. This is party timing on paper. A flow sheet simply says who does what when. It's the party script. Without it no one knows when to do what. Divide up the work on a party flow sheet and assign jobs to yourself and your assistant. Mark off jobs when completed. That way you won't forget anything. Whether I have one assistant or ten for a job, I send everyone a party flow sheet in the mail. They get it about five days before the party. This saves time and fosters the behavior I want in the people I hire. If I don't take the time to tell my staff clearly and precisely what I want them to do, who will?

Here's what I include in a party flow sheet for every staff member:

- Correct party date
- Location, address with map attached, and parking details
- Where I can be reached and what time I'll be at the location
- My phone numbers
- What staff members are to wear and where to put a change of clothes
- Their call time (the time they are to arrive) and their job from the moment they arrive throughout the evening
- Timing of the party: when guests arrive, when food is served, and when the wrap-up starts
- How many guests to expect, type of occasion, and what kind of service
- Menu description
- When they will get a break and dinner
- What time I think they will be finished
- Why this party is important to my company
- Why their attitude is important to the party
- When their check will be ready for pickup
- Why I appreciate their help

The more information you share with assistants or staff, the easier it is for them to live up to your expectations. If my clients have concerns about strangers coming to work in their home, I send them a copy of the party flow sheet. It puts their fears at rest knowing that my staff is directed by me and that I am responsible.

Most of the staff I work with today have worked with me

for years. We like and respect one another. My goal is to make it as easy as possible for my staff to do what I need them to do. We make entertaining look easy.

Arranging Transportation and Packing Out Your Party

If you have catered even one party, you have already confronted the urge to lug everything you own to the party and then lug it all back. Try not to bring anything you aren't going to use. Buy the smaller size of staples such as film or foil wrap. Make it as easy as possible to pack and unpack. Twelve hours after your day began, you won't want problems repacking the van.

My partner and I established a standard equipment checklist. Then we customized it on the computer with the menu for every party. Not only did the checklist keep us from forgetting something, it stopped us from bringing anything unnecessary.

Stand next to the van and don't put anything in without checking it off on your list. Careful packing saves you tons of trouble at the site and potential problems with the food en route. (When carrying liquids, sauces, or soup, tape the lid of the container to the bottom with masking tape, so that the contents can't spill.)

One way to organize is to clearly label or color-code food on the menu with small colored self-adhesive dots widely available at office-supply stores. Any food to be served before dinner might be marked with pink dots; food to be prepared and served with the entrée might be marked with green dots; any products served for dessert might get orange dots. (This system really works well if you have two parties in one day.) If you've started your cooking several days in advance, use these dots in all three phases of production: ordering, prepping, and transportation.

On pages 152–53 is an example of a food and equipment pack-out list for a Mexican-theme wedding for one hundred guests, serving appetizers only.

The decision to rent a van or a refrigerated truck depends on the size of your party and what the location is like. Usually a van does nicely. (Add $1.00 per person to your menu price for parties of fifty people or more to pay for the van rental.) Rent from companies that promise roadside service in case of a breakdown.

Vans with double doors that slide make packing and unpacking easier. If you are working out of a small kitchen, the van can double as your pantry or refrigerator on the site. Bring in products as you need them. Cook from course to course, using your coolers or hot boxes stored in the van.

In an effort to make the day of the event less stressful, rent your van for two days. Get it the morning before the event and pack all the dry goods and equipment first. Be sure to leave room for the food. Then when you get to the site, reverse the process. Unpack the food first, ensuring proper food handling and temperature control. Then off-load dry goods, equipment, or linens in the order you'll use them.

Food handling is a big responsibility. I always ask my clients to empty their refrigerators before the party so that I can use every inch. I also order 100 extra pounds of ice with the liquor order to replenish ice in any coolers I've brought.

If you don't know about correct food handling, it's imperative to learn. Cold food must stay below $45°$; hot food must stay at $145°$ or above; otherwise the food enters a danger zone where bacteria multiply rapidly. In chapter 2 I recommended asking your local health department for written advice and guidelines. I also suggest contacting the Education Foundation of the National Restaurant Association, Chicago, IL 60606, and requesting a copy of *Applied Foodservice Sanitation*, an excellent reference book for professionals.

Getting Down to the Wire

During the days before the party, it's important to keep in close contact with your client. You may be confident, organized, and prepared, but the client is probably a nervous wreck as the day approaches. Nothing calms a client down better than knowing that you are on top of details.

Look for ways to make the day of the event as simple as

Party Pack-Out checklist

Date:_____

Party address: _____

(Check off with initials)

Menu items	Prepped	Wrapped	On the truck
jalapeño cheese palmiers	_____	_____	_____
mushroom olive empanaditas	_____	_____	_____
macho quesedillas	_____	_____	_____
flour tortillas, smoked chicken	_____	_____	_____
refried beans	_____	_____	_____
nachos	_____	_____	_____
tortilla chips, cheese	_____	_____	_____
salsa, green onion	_____	_____	_____
sour cream, jalapeños	_____	_____	_____
crudités basket	_____	_____	_____
black bean dip, guacamole	_____	_____	_____
seafood brochettes	_____	_____	_____
chicken brochettes	_____	_____	_____
tomatillo sauce	_____	_____	_____
seafood bar	_____	_____	_____
steamed clams, mussels	_____	_____	_____
scallop seviche	_____	_____	_____
salsa, sour cream	_____	_____	_____
round tortilla chips	_____	_____	_____
spice kit, cilantro	_____	_____	_____
oil for frying	_____	_____	_____
fresh fruit display	_____	_____	_____
wedding cake cookies	_____	_____	_____
lemon and lime wedges	_____	_____	_____
coffee, tea	_____	_____	_____
half and half, creamer	_____	_____	_____
sugar, artificial substitute	_____	_____	_____

	Prepped	Wrapped	On the truck
(Check off with initials)			
Garnish, Decor, Props			
cactus leaves, pepper ropes	_____	_____	_____
whole onions, kale	_____	_____	_____
sombreros, clay pots	_____	_____	_____
risers, piñatas, terra-cotta trays	_____	_____	_____
Equipment			
spatulas	_____	_____	_____
wooden spoons	_____	_____	_____
tongs	_____	_____	_____
plastic wrap and foil	_____	_____	_____
first-aid kit	_____	_____	_____
fire extinguisher	_____	_____	_____
slotted spoons	_____	_____	_____
sheet pans	_____	_____	_____
oven mitts	_____	_____	_____
whisk and ladles	_____	_____	_____
oyster shucker	_____	_____	_____
paper towels	_____	_____	_____
trash bags	_____	_____	_____
sponge and detergent	_____	_____	_____
Sterno	_____	_____	_____
aprons and towels	_____	_____	_____
ashtrays	_____	_____	_____
assorted baskets	_____	_____	_____
knife roll	_____	_____	_____
serving bowls	_____	_____	_____
corkscrew	_____	_____	_____
cutting boards	_____	_____	_____
pitchers	_____	_____	_____
toothpicks	_____	_____	_____

possible. If you're working in a private home or at a location that allows deliveries the day before the event, have your rentals or dry goods or even the flowers arrive then. You can meet the delivery people there, recheck your orders, and even put some pieces of the party in place.

I like to ask for a spot where I can leave a basketful of brochures, business cards, or matchbooks. I also like to squirrel away a party folder with extra copies of the menu, staff sign-in sheets (to verify the time the staff arrives and departs, for payroll purposes), and party instructions. I make sure to leave the client my phone number and an estimated schedule of the time the staff and subcontractors will arrive.

Another task I like to complete the day before is to set up a mini-recycling station for bottles, cans, and plastic so that it will be easy for anyone working the party to help me recycle as soon as the party begins. The day before is also the perfect time to walk through the place with the client to find out where the light switches are, the fuse box, the garden hose, or the smoke detectors. Anything you might need to know while on the premises, find out now. I usually get a copy of the guest list or the boxes of the bride's party favors or guest book at this time. (I hate to bother clients with these details when they should be enjoying their party.)

If I plan to give my clients a present of a basketful of goodies or a special bottle of champagne, I do it the day before—I want to be sure the client knows it was from me.

Before the rooms are full of guests is a good time to talk with the host or hostess about where to put coats or baby bags or unexpected gifts or, for that matter, where to put a guest who is ill. This is the moment to talk about putting away any irreplaceable household items. If you are using the client's equipment, you'll want to jot down a list to make sure it gets put back where it belongs.

Finally, remind the client about film or batteries for his or her camera. He or she will thank you later and think you are a genius.

In chapter 9, Pulling It Off with Ease, you'll see how all your organizing techniques and checklists work. Whether you want to admit it or not, how well the party comes off is a direct reflection of your preplanning, communication skills, and attitude. I am not saying that you can control everything. There are four legitimate exceptions: monsoons, flu epidemics, union strikes, and war. But as a professional caterer, you'll be expected to handle just about everything else.

9

Pulling It Off with Ease

Doing as much work as you can on a job beforehand makes pulling it off, well, a piece of cake. If you can get more than half the work done before the event, you can't help but feel confident the big day itself. By working ahead you give yourself the gift of self-assurance, a gift that clients and staff feel, too. Like the coach of a winning team, you need to provide inspiration as well as guidance and controls on party day.

The Day of the Party

Get a good night's sleep the night before. The better you take care of yourself, the more patience and strength you will have to cope with the unexpected. Put on comfortable clothes, support hose (men, too), and walking shoes. Plan on changing into party clothes, or at least a clean chef's jacket, before the guests arrive. One thing I hate to see is staff or kitchen help walking through a party in dirty uniforms or casual clothes. Do they believe they are invisible? Who could miss them? Imagine a stagehand walking through a classical ballet performance wearing a sweatshirt and baseball cap! Good catering is like good dancing: The audience must never see you sweat.

Attention to detail and the ability to see your parties as a performance, not a perfunctory job, are two things that set you apart from your competition. To achieve that professional smoothness, make day-of-the-party lists like this one. It covers every aspect of the party for which you are responsible.

Master Checklist

Party Information Folder / Your Paperwork

- [ ] Copy of completed and signed contract
- [ ] Date and final guest count given by client
- [ ] Copy of deposit and balance checks, in case client has a question
- [ ] Subcontractors' contracts and phone numbers
- [ ] Staff phone numbers, addresses, and arrival times
- [ ] Staff payroll sheet for sign-in and out
- [ ] Priority job list or special instructions for all staff
- [ ] Copies of special fire permits, if necessary, and a certificate of insurance
- [ ] Several copies of final menu—one for kitchen staff, one for waiters, one for bartenders—all staff briefed to answer guests' questions
- [ ] Printed instructions on the sequence of food courses, timing, and type of service
- [ ] Diagram of how to set up temporary kitchen and organize existing space
- [ ] Copy of rental orders
- [ ] List of customer's equipment that will be used
- [ ] Entire location layout: placement of bar, food displays, kitchen area, scullery, guest tables and chairs, coatrack, place for gifts, security, barbecue, trash, recycling, fire extinquishers
- [ ] Rental company's conditions of equipment return (what must or must not be washed)

☐ Instructions for repacking food for kitchen crew and wait staff
☐ Blank party-closing reports (staff feedback sheet) to delegate to two staff members

Transportation Checklist
☐ Van gassed; map of location; food, supplies, and equipment checked off and packed
☐ Rental-van keys or car keys on huge, colored key ring, impossible to misplace

Menu
☐ All menu items color-coded to menu courses, tightly wrapped for transport, and packed in coolers, hot boxes, or crates
☐ Special cooking instructions or finishing details attached to appropriate ingredients with tape
☐ Signs to hang up for each course or food station telling which area waiters are to use to pick up appetizers, salads, or desserts
☐ Appointment of buffet monitors to replenish from backup food supply

Equipment Placement / Breakdown Instructions
☐ Scullery supplies, dishwasher, plastic bags for napkins, soap, rubber gloves, bus tubs for dirty dishes, flatware cleaner, sponges, garbage cans, table for repacking, running water. (Note: Not all of these items will be needed if the job is at a private home.)
☐ Breakdown of rentals for storage, packing, and security until pickup
☐ Pack broom, mop and garbage can on van in case they are not available at location.
☐ Appointed hours for cleanup of premises and next-day inspection

Service Staff / Evaluations / Employee Information
☐ Appoint one member of the wait staff to be your assistant and help you pass information to other staff as well as fill out party-closing report.

☐ Pack emergency toilet articles appearance bag: one extra bow tie, hair spray, panty hose, safety pins, hair brush, lint brush, portable iron, black shoe polish, deodorant, extra chef's jacket, perfume, mouthwash, portable razor, belt, portable sewing kit, aspirin, and tampons.

☐ Designate place for staff's purses or jackets and decide chain of command for breaks and meals. Set aside fruit or sandwiches for snacking and water.

☐ Post job assignments and list of staff arrival times in designated area.

☐ Post copy of menu with all ingredients listed and instructions for staff to initial after reading.

☐ Post description of service buffet stations, sit-down or combination.

☐ Post special instructions such as cutting and passing the wedding cake, security of presents, where coats go, scullery duties.

☐ Allow ten minutes for preparty meeting with staff to answer questions about party and potential problems and at least three minutes for inspirational message about what you envision from this team effort.

☐ Appoint two bathroom monitors to check bathrooms every thirty minutes for toilet paper and towels. Monitors must know where the plunger is, too (most toilets in private homes aren't used to being flushed one hundred times in four hours. Crowds create plumbing problems).

Getting to the Party

Allow enough time to get to the party without racing. Have clear and concise directions and a map. A cellular phone is a time-saving tool because it enables a caterer to be on tap every minute for questions, to handle surprises, or even just to call the client and say, "I'm on my way."

If you work from a copy of your master checklist and your party-information file, it will be difficult for you to put the wrong foot forward. I can't emphasize too often that the success of the party depends on hours of preplanning and anticipating possible problems.

On the day of the party, caterers sometimes make the mistake of going back to the kitchen or to the store for one forgotten item. This leaves the staff at the party site without a leader and without instructions. If you've forgotten the toothpicks with color-coordinated frills, either do without them or send someone else to find them. The coach is too important to leave the game on an errand.

Even with careful scheduling, mishaps occur. If a purveyor is late with a delivery to your kitchen the morning of the party, don't hold up the entire parade. Call and find out if the delivery can be made right to the party site, or decide if you should leave a kitchen assistant behind to accept the delivery. Be flexible. Be able to manage your time. Perhaps the item is for dessert and you have some time before you need it. Know that there is no problem you can't solve. Just think through each dilemma.

I've managed to solve some very thorny problems, and I know that you can, too. Once I was the executive chef in charge of a celebrity wedding on the island of Catalina. All the food had to be coordinated, prepped, weighed, wrapped, then sent on a barge the day before the wedding. The 150 guests, all television stars, were crossing the 17 miles of water between Los Angeles and Catalina in luxury yachts. At five o'clock on the morning of the wedding, just as I was leaving the house for the helicopter pad to fly to the island, the phone rang. It was the baker of the wedding cake, who said she had missed the barge. This was summer. The yachts and other passenger boats were booked full. The baker was sorry, but she didn't know how she could get the four-tiered wedding cake to Catalina.

I told her to meet me at the helicopter pad. The helicopter carried only four passengers and there was no storage space, but I figured I could manage. As the wind from the copter's blades blew the baker and me around, I passed the first two tiers of the cake to total strangers in the helicopter screaming, "Would you mind holding this for a minute?" My assistant and I took the last two tiers and climbed aboard. The ride took thirty-seven minutes. I smiled the entire time, looking straight into the innocent faces of my fellow passengers, all holding tiers of wedding cake. They said not a word. Neither did I. When we landed, I climbed out, took the cake from their tired arms, said my thank yous, and put the cake in a waiting taxi.

Arriving at the Party Site

It's a good idea to get to the party before any of your staff. If they are standing there waiting for you, it's costing you money.

Make a job-priority list (see the example on pages 164–65) that contains names of staff by each job with written instructions for everything. Post the list in a prominent place so that all staff can refer to it. As each staff member completes a task, he or she checks it and initials it before moving on to the next.

A job-priority list is a form of delegation. I need to know that my staff won't need me every second. I may need to be on the phone finishing instructions about a party the next day or answering another set of nervous questions by the bride's mother or trying to find a place for the family dogs away from the barbecue while the chef is grilling burgers.

A job-priority list is also a systematic way of making sure that your party is ready when the guests arrive, that you are using your staff effectively, and that you have left time for yourself to take pictures or to be available in case your client needs you.

It also keeps your party on schedule.

Winding Down: Why Your Party Has to End on Time

To stay within your budget, you need to stick to the time schedule you laid out in your contract. If the contract called for a four-hour party, give your client four hours, not four and a half. As the guests start through the sequence of events—cocktails, dining, dancing—you and your staff should be cleaning up behind them. Service the client, serve the food, and start to repack in an effort to organize the breakdown as the party winds down. For example, once the appetizers have been served, have someone repack any leftovers into the ice chests, clean the trays, and put all equipment you brought for the appetizers back on the truck. Clean up your party and repack as you go along.

Occasionally you'll encounter guests who don't want to leave even when the party is over. You'll have to enlist your host and explain that your job is done. If the client wants the bartender to stay another hour, you can, of course, agree, but only if the client is willing to pay extra for the bartender's time. Remember that you have to pay for every minute your staff works, whether you collected the correct amount of dollars from your client or not.

Report Cards from Staff and Clients

The easiest way to get honest feedback and to document the results of your parties is to develop party-closing reports (see pages 166–67). I think of them as report cards. Ask two staff members, one from the floor, one from the kitchen, to each fill out a closing report the day of the party. I ask each client to fill one out a couple of days later. These reports make it simple to see and correct mistakes in order to perfect your home-base catering business.

How a Staff Report Works

For example, if after two parties in a row your kitchen assistant says that he didn't have any pot holders, do the following: (1) Go back to your equipment pack-out list and verify whether or not you packed them; (2) determine whether your kitchen assistant is looking in the wrong box; and (3) determine whether the pot holders got left at another party.

If you learn that your staff felt rushed when the guests arrived, you know that you need to rethink timing. Either you are

Job Assignments

Write your initials in the appropriate blanks as you complete each task.

☐	Carol	Check rental delivery against the delivery sheet.
☐	Michael	Put every piece of equipment in place.
☐	Carol	Pass out linens, drape them, and roll silverware or fold napkins.
☐	Marie	Refrigerate food.
☐	Marie	Verify deliveries from outside suppliers.
☐	Gary	Make sure bar supplies are adequate and ready for first guests.
☐	Denise	Meet with waiters to discuss menu and party timing.
☐	Marie	Build salad and have appetizers ready.
☐	Michael	Be ready to meet early arrivals dressed in your waiter's uniform.
☐	Gary	Make sure that all caterer's equipment is out of sight.
☐	Michael	Greet guests, handle guest book sign-in.
☐	Carol	Escort guests to their tables.
☐	Denise	Seat wedding party at bride's table.
☐	Marie	Finish beef in oven.
☐	Denise	Tell disk jockey to announce when the buffet will open.
☐	Marie	Take carving knife to buffet.
☐	Michael	Place bread baskets and butter curls on all tables.
☐	Gary	Fill water glasses and add lemon slice.

	Assigned To	Task
☐	Gary	Pour champagne into flutes for toast at 3:00 P.M.
☐	Michael and Gary	Bus dishes and glasses to scullery.
☐	Carol and Marie	Break down buffet at 4:15 P.M.
☐	Gary	Continue to pour champagne from bar.
☐	Michael and Carol	Cut and serve wedding cake.
☐	Gary	Set up coffee station.
☐	Marie	Wrap all leftover food.
☐	Marie	Feed staff and subcontractors.
☐	Marie	Separate rentals; store in safe place.
☐	Gary	Close bar at 5:00 P.M.
☐	Carol	Help family with gifts to car.
☐	Denise	Pass out bride's candy party favors for departing guests.
☐	Marie	Wrap extra wedding cake for bride's mother.
☐	Anybody not otherwise occupied	Reload van.
☐	Michael	Mop floors.
☐	Denise	Fill out staff time sheets.
☐	Carol	Fill out party-closing sheet.
☐	Marie	Fill out party-closing sheet for kitchen.
☐	Gary	Check location for any equipment.
☐	Anybody not otherwise occupied	Help repack van with equipment and recycling.

Party-Closing Report/Staff Evaluation

Event _____ Date _____

Actual guest count _____ Filled out by _____

Staff on duty _____

_____

1. Was client happy? _____
   Explain _____

2. Did problems arise that the client was aware of? _____
   If so, who handled the problems? _____
   How were the problems handled? _____

3. Were there problems with subcontractors? _____
   Explain _____

4. Would you hire these suppliers again? _____

5. Did the event start on time? _____
   If not, why? _____

6. Was the staff ready on time? _____

7. Did the event go overtime? _____
   Why? _____

8. Was there enough food for guests and staff? _____
   If not, what did we run out of? _____

9. Were there any complaints? _____
   Explain: _____

10. Were there any injuries to staff or clients? _____
    Explain: _____

11. Did you discuss these injuries with the host or hostess? _____

12. Evaluate the organization of this party and how I did as coordinator. _____
    _____

13. How would you rate your fellow service staff? _____

14. Were there any personality conflicts among staff members? _____

15. Were staff members clear about their responsibilities? _____

16. Could you suggest anything that might make it easier for all of us next time? _____
    _____

not allowing enough time for the set up, or your staff needs clearer directions so that they don't waste time; or you are cutting it too close and you need another pair of hands to help.

Staff reports are particularly valuable if you have two parties on the same day and you can only get to one of them. You'll want to be informed about everything, good or bad, before you ask your client to fill out a report card and give you referrals.

Also, several months later, when the details of a party are fuzzy at best, staff reports may protect you from an employee or a guest who complains of an injury after the fact. You will be able to produce paperwork showing that no injury was reported at the time or that you took steps to gather information about any accidents with the intention of dealing with them.

I had a wonderful employee call me forty days after a party to say that he'd wrenched his back lifting a table and was filing a worker's compensation claim. When I checked my computer index for that date, I discovered that not only had he not worked for me then, but I didn't even have a party that day. It isn't unusual during the busy season for professional waiters to work for four different caterers in one week. In the time that had elapsed since his injury, he remembered the wrong caterer.

Asking for honest feedback from a client is harder than asking for it from staff. After the energy, effort, and anxiety you've put into an event, you want to believe that your performance was flawless. You don't want to hear anything but praise. This attitude can work against you. To get over this I learned to take responsibility for my actions as a professional. At the end of a party, if I felt that I had worked my butt off and not made enough profit, I had no one to blame but myself—I couldn't blame the client. I had not protected myself and educated the client about what was best for both of us, so I could not be angry with him or her.

I meet caterers all the time who are unable to turn a negative into a positive. Their inability to admit a mistake and learn from it contributes to burnout, dissatisfaction, and frustration in their jobs. They don't feel that clients appreciate what they do, yet they can't handle critiques that would improve their performances. I suggest that they refer to their contracts and ask themselves these questions: Did I do what the client expected and paid for, or did I do things I wanted and maybe not what the client paid for? Am I angry at the client or at myself? Is my perfectionism working against me? Without a good look at what they have done, I'll bet dollars to doughnuts they make the same mistakes over and over again.

You need perspective about each of your performances, and sometimes it's hard to look at a party honestly when your back still aches from all that cooking the night before. The client's party-closing report will help you clarify both your thinking and your client's about the final results of the event. When you are honest with yourself, trust me, the complaints are few and far between, and the ones you do get are useful.

On pages 170–71 is a sample questionnaire to send to your client after the party.

The Day After

How you feel the day after may depend on how much natural energy you have and how well your party planning worked. Because you are your own boss, you can rest whenever it is best for you. In December it's common for small companies, big companies, or any company to work nonstop for three or four days or weeks in a row. It becomes a habit, and your body gets on a roll. You are exhausted by Christmas. You expect to be, but you made enough money to support yourself in January, a slow month for caterers.

In my house the day after any party is a day of rest. I'm tired and exhilarated. I bask in the glory of my achievement. I reflect on how I would do the same party again, but better and more profitably. I make notes in red pen on my master checklist of items and circle things I wouldn't do again. I scribble notes to myself about the menu, staff, equipment, and suppliers while the facts are all fresh in my mind. This takes me thirty minutes, tops.

I review the closing reports carefully and try to make decisions that will eliminate problems in future parties. On the back

Quality and Service Report

1. Are you glad that you were referred to my company? _____

2. Did you feel that I explained my policies promptly and courteously when we went over the menu package and party proposal? _____

3. From our meetings and discussions, do you feel as though you received the party you were promised? _____

4. Are you satisfied that we completed our contractual agreement? _____
_____

5. Was the quality of the food as good as I promised? _____
Did you enjoy it? _____

6. Which dish was your favorite? _____

7. Did the food presentation meet your expectations? _____

8. Did you receive compliments from your guests? _____

9. Was the temperature of each dish correct? _____

10. Do you feel that you got value for your dollars? _____

11. On a scale of 1 to 10, please rate the service staff. _____

12. Were there any problems I should know about that you are reluctant to bring up? _____

13. Was your home or the party site left in satisfactory condition? _____

14. Please tell me anything you feel would enable me to serve you better next time. _____

15. May I use your name as a reference? _____

16. Would you be comfortable writing me a letter of recommendation? _____

Please mention what you liked best about working with me. _____

17. Please list below the names of three friends or colleagues who might need my services in the future. _____

_____

_____

Thanks again. I hope I have the opportunity to do another party for you in the future.

Remember: Referral and repeat business comes with client satisfaction.

of the reports, I list the pieces of the party that I loved and was proud of: for example, the decor was charming, the food was fresh and tasty, my staff worked hard and looked great. I take the time to savor what satisfied me as an owner, a businessperson, a chef, and an artist.

I've learned to hear and accept the compliments without adding "Yes, but . . . " or "Well, I'm glad you enjoyed the six-course dinner, but I wish the rolls had been a little bit warmer." Strive for excellence, not perfection.

If, in a tense moment, I wasn't the perfect manager, coach, player, or boss, I ask myself if I owe anyone an apology. If so, I call them. I also ask myself whether I'm owed an apology. If so, does it really matter if I get one?

If during this reinspection of the event, I decide that there was misconduct on the part of an employee, I make a note in that person's folder and decide if I should speak to him or her about it. Accidents are accidents and mistakes are mistakes, but neglect is grounds for dismissal.

Two Days Later

Send your client a Quality and Service Report questionnaire in the mail. If you haven't talked to him or her since the party, now's the time. Call and tell your client to look forward to the questionnaire and explain why you're sending it. Enclose a stamped, self-addressed envelope and a handwritten thank-you note.

If there are loose ends, tie them up. Does the client owe you for two dinners? Send an invoice for them separately. Did you pick up the client's spatula by mistake? Tell the client what day you'll drop it off. Do you need to go to the location to verify a burn mark on the table from your chafer or a steam mark on a painting from your coffeepot?

If there is any damage, call your insurance agent, take a Polaroid picture of the item, find out what your deductible is, negotiate the value of the damage, and be done with it. A hundred dollars to fix a problem when it involves a client who may send you thousands of dollars in business is an easy solution.

Write thank-you notes to any purveyor or supplier who helped you—the butcher, the baker, the band. Many busy businesspeople forget how important a sincere thank-you can be.

Do your bookkeeping and accounting now. As we discussed in chapter 7, bookkeeping is easy if you do a little every day, like exercise and flossing your teeth. Figure your final party profit sheet. Take a blank budget worksheet like the one we used in chapter 5 and insert your actual costs. It's a great way to see how close you came to your estimates. Most new home-based caterers quickly get the hang of judging food quantities, but bidding correctly on labor costs takes experience. You have to be able to visualize parties, know what each staff position does, and how parties flow before you will be able to stop underbidding labor costs and stop working yourself to death.

Pay your purveyors, your staff, yourself. Organize all the information you have in your party folder: staff sheets, final accounting sheet, recipes to document the menu. A copy of the original proposal and your closing party reports belong here, too. Any information that applies to the party goes in the party folder: the rental order, the purveyors you used, the store where you bought the balloons, the bid from the designer who built the incredible archway. Why keep all this paper? Because if the party was as good as you think it was and it received glowing reviews, a guest from that party may call and order one just like it. By reselling a party you can make more money with less stress. Most of your planning has been done and you know your costs to the penny. Catering parties is like making crepes: the more you make, the better your pan gets.

For you to resell this party now, with all that you know, would be like taking candy from a baby.

Three Days Later

After you've done your bookkeeping, call your staff and tell them when their paychecks will be ready. Thank them again for their support and talent. It's a good time to ask each one what he or she thought of the party, the food, and the guests' reaction.

Listen and look at your party through their eyes. Know that many of the waiters you hire also work with your competitors. They know a lot about the catering clientele in your area. Staff is a great source of information and insight.

Call the rental company and make sure that all its property was picked up properly and that your account is clear. If the company has complaints, now is the time to answer them.

One classic complaint of rental companies concerns napkins. The number of cloth napkins rented is never the same as the number returned. When the rental company sends you an invoice at the end of the month, it always charges you $5.00 a napkin, or whatever its replacement cost may be. Calculate how much money you will spend during two years in business if you lose between two and five napkins at each party.

Here's how it happens. One napkin went into the garbage can because the new prep cook grabbed it (he didn't know where the kitchen towels were) to clean the client's incredibly dirty grill. When he saw the mess he made of the napkin, he buried his mistake in the garbage can. Kiss that one good-bye. Another napkin was left in the hostess's bathroom by a guest, so the hostess keeps it next to her phone to remind her the next time she calls you. The third napkin is in one of your waiter's cars. His defroster wasn't working, so he took it when he left the party to wipe off his windshield.

You get my drift. It's important to stress to the staff the value of rental equipment. Count the rentals when you arrive. Count the rentals when you pack up to leave, and get the staff to help you account for them. Be sure to explain exactly how much replacements cost.

Two Weeks Later

Contact the three leads from your client's Quality and Service Report. Write each lead a cover letter. If you have a recent promotional piece, a descriptive menu from a charity fund-raiser, a free recipe card, or a copy of your newsletter, enclose it along with your standard marketing package. Ask each of the three leads if he or she was at the party. If so, they know a lot about you already. Your goal is to make an appointment with all three of them to talk about future jobs. You'll make back the price of a cup of coffee and a brownie many times over.

Pick up the film you dropped off the day after the party. Select the best shots from the two sets of pictures you had printed and give a set of them to your client. I enclose the pictures with a business card and put them directly in the client's mailbox. I call two days later to ask if they got the pictures and if they liked them. Again I tell them how much I appreciate their business. I'm from the school that says you can't be too considerate or too thoughtful to clients.

Go to the stationery store and buy shiny gold stars just like the ones you were given in kindergarten. On every calendar in your life—in your organizer, on your desk calendar—stick those stars on the dates of every party you complete. Put them wherever you can to remind yourself that you are accomplishing your goals and living your dream.

Looking back on ten years of catering, I know I wouldn't have missed a single party. Even the parties that made me cry, forced me to admit mistakes, and "built my character" were worth it.

I feel a real sense of accomplishment and joy when I see a near-perfect party come together because of my ideas and designs. To start with a vacant buffet or empty backyard and, in a few hours, create an entirely new fairy-tale setting and wonderful memories—and then get paid for it— still seems to me a miracle.

10
Solving Problems
The Twelve Questions
New Caterers Most Often Ask

After you've catered three or four parties, I can anticipate the problems you'll be having. I know. I've been there. Apparently you aren't alone because these are the questions I am asked repeatedly when teaching.

The most important advice I can give you is to try not to make the same mistakes twice. Learn from your experience, tuck the knowledge away, and use it when planning the next time.

Question One

I called my client the day before the party, and she gave me her final guest count. At the party twenty more guests arrived, and I ran out of rolls and salad. Fortunately I had lots of roast beef and shrimp to feed them. What should I do differently next time?

• In your sales presentation be even firmer when addressing

your need for an accurate guest count. Make sure the client understands that she will pay for every guest you feed, even if the guests are a surprise to everyone. You are only trying to ensure her success as a hostess.

- When guests arrive, it's important to have someone at the door counting. The earlier you know about a soaring guest count, the sooner you can send someone to the store.
- Salad and bread are the cheapest items on your menu. You need to figure one and one-half rolls per person for a buffet, at least two for a sit-down dinner. Better to bring a few extra rolls than 10 extra pounds of roast beef (two dozen rolls cost $3.00; 10 pounds of roast beef cost about $30). Remember that if you buy too many rolls, you can use the leftovers to make great bread crumbs, bread pudding, or croutons for Caesar salad.
- Instead of running out of rolls, you could have cut the existing rolls in half when you refilled the bread basket.
- If you ever begin to run short of salad or any other self-service item, put a waiter on the buffet to serve it. He will control the portions and make it stretch.
- As a last resort, look in the refrigerator of the hostess to see if she has any lettuce. Or does she have a garden in the backyard? You can replace the items you use later.

Question Two

No matter how organized I try to be, I always forget one or two items. What can I do?

- Are you making lists? Or trying to remember details in your head instead? The latter is a no-no. Be sure to make foolproof prep lists and equipment lists from your menus. Mark off each item as you pack it in your car or van.
- Put together an on-site box for yourself. Keep it stocked and bring it to every party. Pack the following items: wooden matches, sugar cubes, toothpicks, dry coffee creamer, herb tea bags, pot holders, plastic food-storage bags, doilies, bamboo skewers, a small fire extinguisher, and a box of birthday candles. Add the things you have been forgetting.

- Designate a backup driver or "gofer" for your party. It can be a neighbor or teenager whom you pay for a few hours to sit next to the phone and be available to bring you anything you've forgotten.
- Allow enough time to pack out your party. The less stress you are under, the easier it is to remember.
- Delegate: When you think of items you keep forgetting, ask someone else—a staff or family member—to help you remember next time.
- Schedule your waiter to call you at the party site before arrival. He or she can pick up the things you've forgotten.

Question Three

I've been afraid to do anything but the food for my caterings, but recently I've noticed I come up with more ideas than the wedding consultants or the party planners that hire me. How can I make more money?

You should definitely try your hand at the flowers and the decor to easily increase your profits. Let me give you an example from my own experience.

I was catering a beach wedding. The bride's florist wanted $35 per table for fifteen arrangements of tropical plants. Knowing that the budget was tight, I suggested to the bride that she consider using sand, shells, and two goldfish in a bowl on every table. She loved the idea. In the end each table cost me $6.00 to decorate—I charged $18. Everybody was happy: The bride spent half as much as she expected, and I made $180 for an hour's work and a good idea.

I used the same process I use in menu pricing to calculate my price. I estimated what my costs would be, analyzed the labor, was flexible, and budgeted my profit on a worksheet.

Selling centerpieces or getting involved in other aspects of the party planning can be a lifesaver if you discover that you've underpriced a menu. In my experience even the best prepared caterer sometimes makes a mistake or quotes a menu price that's too low. In that case see whether you can interest your client in some wonderful centerpieces or a fabulous balloon sculpture or two singing waiters. The money you make in "upselling" the client this way may make the difference between a party that puts you in the black and one that puts you in the red.

Question Four

My food tastes great and I love to cook, but I'm not good at setting up my buffets. Are there any tricks I can learn for presentation that don't cost a lot of money?

Here are twelve tips for effective buffet presentation:

Tip 1. Use different sizes, colors, and textures of cloth as accent overlays with banquet rental cloths. Drape the tablecloths to the floor to cover the table legs. Buy the swatches of cloth at close-outs in fabric stores. I've even used twin-sized sheets in various patterns that I bought at a white sale as overlays.

Tip 2. Create height. Elevate food with plastic risers or glass bricks (available at a builder's supply store). Votive candles behind the bricks create a wonderful light at night. Crates and boxes, even stacks of paper plates hidden under the cloth overlays, also add height.

Tip 3. For free risers cover empty coffee cans with faux-marble contact paper and put trays across the top for a dramatic high-tech look. I've also used tall terra-cotta pots turned on their sides with a napkin liner to serve tortilla chips and Mexican bread.

Tip 4. Place cheese and fruit on mirrored squares or broken pieces of marble from a hardware store or a marble quarry. Line different-shaped baskets with aromatic herbs to serve bread. Put salads in glass bowls to show off the colors.

Tip 5. Spray paint is the recycler of props. I own baskets that have been gold, black, red, or whatever color I needed. I go over them with a wire brush for a burnished look and then spray them again.

Tip 6. Mix copper and silver chafing dishes, oblong with round. I've found antique-looking serving pieces at garage sales for less than $20 each.

Tip 7. Look around your garage or at garage sales for junk that can be used as props. An old fish bowl might be perfect on a Chinese stir-fry display, with one goldfish, or koi, as the center of attention.

Tip 8. Have your florist make two or three different-shaped arrangements instead of one standard buffet piece. Stagger the arrangements or group them on pillars behind the buffet. Or hang them from a beam behind the buffet. Or have a garland made and snake it through the chafing dishes. Ask your florist to give you any broken-stemmed flowers for free to scatter on the dessert table. Imagination is all it takes.

Tip 9. Tier candles in different-shaped holders. (Before you do this, be sure that props and cloths are fire retardant, and check local fire codes.) Use colored bulbs in ceiling lights or hang spotlights or Chinese lanterns. You can buy gel paper at photography stores to color lights, too.

Tip 10. Have your client rent battery-pack neon lights to highlight floral arrangements.

Tip 11. Dress your food servers in ethnic costumes to complement your theme or buffet. Coordinate your outfit to the color scheme. (I look great in peach, so I push that color theme.)

Tip 12. Rent sound effects from special-effect companies. Running water or a babbling brook under an Oriental display conjures up a Japanese garden.

Question Five

I get a lot of calls for jobs I have to turn away because I have only one pair of hands and I don't know how to handle volume. Do you have any suggestions?

Try not to turn away business. Try to solve the client's problems or work with another caterer or food source to pull the job off. At the very least you should be able to find another caterer and refer the job to him. Then ask for a finder's fee or barter a favor in return.

An example: Recently a caterer I know had a problem. Her client wanted 500 box lunches at $5.00 each. The caterer figured that with overtime pay for helpers working all night and the small amount of refrigeration in her kitchen, it was an impossible feat for her.

I asked her what kind of box lunches her client wanted. "Oh, anything," she said. "Anything that tastes good. She doesn't really care."

In a shopping mall the week before, I saw a sign in a bakery window advertising box lunches for $3.99. I suggested to the caterer that she call the bakery. For an order that large, the bakery agreed to do boxes for $3.50 and to add an orange to the fresh croissant turkey sandwich, pasta salad, and cookie. The manager even agreed to deliver the boxes to the location in a refrigerated van. The caterer asked the bakery to leave its sticker off each box so that she could add hers and enclose a business card. She made $1.50 profit on each box lunch before taxes. The bakery was delighted with the order, the client got a wonderful lunch at the price she wanted to pay, and everyone lived happily ever after.

This was one smart business deal that worked in every way and took only one phone call.

Question Six

I was so careful ordering my rentals, but I still ran out of glasses, dinner plates, and cloth napkins at my party. Why?

This is a universal catering problem. You have to plan on guests' using about five glasses each for an average four-hour party. They do not hold onto the same glass. Every time they go to the bar, even if it's only for mineral water, guests get a clean glass.

Here are some solutions:

Glasses

- Rent five glasses per guest. Charge the client for them.
- If five glasses per guest cost too much, use glass only for the first two hours of the party; then switch to plastic.
- Be prepared to wash glasses. Have detergent, gloves, hot water, and someone to wash the dishes standing by, or plan on running the client's dishwasher.

Napkins

- Keep the cloth napkins under lock and key until you are ready to roll the silverware in them or fold them for placement. Chances are your staff grabbed them before the party and used them when they didn't have towels. Bartenders take them for opening wine. Chefs use them for pot holders, waiters for the bread baskets.
- Order twenty extra napkins (about 55 cents a piece) over your guest count and make the staff happy.

Plates

- If you're catering a buffet, plan on one and one-half dinner plates per guest. If your guest count is one hundred, then put 150 plates out. This amount covers guests who come back for seconds, musicians, valets, waiters, and photographers. You want to make a great impression on everyone at the party, even subcontractors. They help build your reputation in the industry.
- Dessert for one hundred guests probably means that you need only 110 plates. People often pass on dessert or even reuse dessert plates, but not dinner plates.

Question Seven

When my rentals arrived, some cups were chipped, linens were faded, and the white chairs were scraped. We got through the party okay, but I was embarrassed. What can I do?

For next time:

- Always keep on hand the twenty-four-hour number (beeper) of your rental representative. Call immediately to discuss the condition of the equipment and ask him or her to send replacement equipment on another truck.
- Demand a credit on the invoice. You feel cheated, and rightly so.
- Look for another rental company and go down to their warehouse to inspect the merchandise.
- Request the best equipment when you place your order and

tell them that your client is particular. Get the owner of the rental company's guarantee over the phone.

Question Eight

Sometimes clients ask me to leave the leftovers or their guests ask if they can take food home. How do I handle that?

Caterers differ on how they handle leftovers. Some leave them with the client. If you do that, I suggest that you leave written instructions on how the food is to be kept so that you don't run into complaints later.

I won't give leftovers to guests to take home for a number of reasons. For one thing my product-liability insurance doesn't protect me once the food is out of my sight. And what happens when the guest who took the leftovers lets the poached salmon salad with dill mayonnaise get warm, eats it, gets sick, misses several days work, and wants to sue me? It takes my valuable time, attorney's costs, and written documentation from my client to prove that he was the only guest who got sick.

My insurance policy extends only through the hours of the party. As far as I'm concerned, the client buys the food only for the time the party is held. Sometimes in my contract I put the specific times the buffet will be open and closed. Not only does this keep the food safe, it also prevents clients from inviting a secret "second shift" to a party if they think you'll leave the buffet up for hours. They hope you won't notice twenty-five extra guests—latecomers—and that they'll eat for free.

Your best bet is to make the right amount of food so that you don't have leftovers after you've served the staff and subcontractors. I've found that leaving leftovers can work against me if the client sees a lot of food and thinks, "Gosh, if Denise hadn't made so much, maybe the party wouldn't have cost so much." Also, if they reheat a product and it doesn't taste good because it's dry and brown, they sometimes wonder if their guests really enjoyed it.

I had a client call me once to ask for a refund on a wedding cake a week after the reception. It seems she had tasted the last bite five days after the wedding and didn't think it tasted fresh-baked. "I was surprised by how dry it was," she told me. "Maybe that's why the guests didn't eat it all."

I told her that since her guests had gone back for seconds and thirds on the buffet (and, incidentally, raved about the entrées), they may have been too full for dessert. I had tasted the cake at the reception and knew it was delicious. When she admitted that she hadn't kept it tightly wrapped, it was easy for me to convince her that it wasn't right for me to give her a refund.

I admit that I'm stricter on this subject than many other caterers, but I work in California, which is a very lawsuit-happy state. I make sure my clients know at the outset that there may not be any leftovers, and that if there are, I won't leave them behind. I have found that they'll agree to anything as long as I tell them my policy at the outset.

Question Nine

My client supplied her own bar, and I hired a professional bartender from a personnel service; still one of the guests got drunk. When I asked the bartender how many drinks he served that guest, he said two, but apparently she drank the complimentary wine on the table during dinner. It was uncomfortable for everyone. Is there is a way to stop this in the future?

This is a serious problem in our industry. You want to be aware of the legal liabilities of your company and think about your moral obligation to the community. Call your local state Alcohol Beverage Control Board and ask about information and brochures they can share with you.

Remember that if a guest has a drinking problem, nothing will stop him or her from getting drunk. Serious drinkers carry small bottles in their purses or jackets. (You find the empties under the tables or in the bathrooms later.) But you can make sure that they don't drive away from the party.

In California that's why valet parking services have become so popular. The valet will not turn over car keys to an intoxicated driver. You can assist by suggesting a cab or by calling the police. This is drastic, but sometimes necessary. At the very least, ask the hostess, who might take the guest home safely.

Here are some additional tips:
- Make some written notes that you alerted and discussed this problem with your client before the party. If you encounter a drunken guest, document what you did about it, too. You may have to take the lead because the host and hostess may have had a couple of drinks, too.
- Get information and brochures on the designated-driver program from your sheriff's department. When you are selling the party, ask the hostess if she would like to offer this to her guests. In each invitation make mention of the program or include a button. Tell them that designated drivers get chocolate-chip cookie bags from the caterer when they leave and free soft drinks during the party.
- I never purchase liquor for my guests or sell it to them. I am happy to supply a suggested bar list or suggest a wine that goes well with the food, but I don't profit from the sale of liquor, nor do I place the order or pay for it.
- Explain to clients that all wine and liquor should be poured and monitored by professional bartenders and wait staff. If staff alerts you to a client who has had enough to drink, stand behind the staff in the decision to stop serving that person.
- Do you know other caterers who are selling liquor to their clients? They may own a liquor license or use one from a restaurant they own—or they may be breaking the law. Check the laws in your state and be sure to stay on the right side of them.

Question Ten

At my last party one of the waiters didn't show up. At the preparty meeting I told all my staff to please work faster. We were shorthanded for the entire party. It made it stressful for everyone, and several of the staff complained. What else could I have done?

This will happen to you more than once in your career. Here are some alternatives to consider:
- The instant you know one waiter is a no-show, ask the other

waiters if they know of anyone they can call to come help solve the problem. Even if he can't arrive for two hours, he'll get there in time to help clear the dinner dishes, lighten clean up, and be a hero.

- Keep a list of wait staff in your organized party folder. Assign one person to start calling until a replacement is found.
- When you schedule your party, ask a waiter to be on call. I've offered people $20 to be on call for the two hours preceding the start of my parties. It works. After two hours if I haven't called, they get the $20 and can do what they like.
- Make it understood when you are hiring staff that if they stand you up and aren't calling from a hospital to report why they are not there, they no longer work for you.
- If you can't reach anyone to help, tell the existing staff that you appreciate the extra effort and you will disburse the pay of the missing waiter among them. A thank-you and up-front incentive work wonders.

Question Eleven

After doing four or five caterings, I am not making enough money. It seems as though I always forget to charge for something or something goes wrong and I have to pay for it. What can I do?

Promise to reread chapters 3, 5, and 7 and stop acting as though you don't understand math or that you are too creative to be bothered about money.

Catering is a business, and I bet you are not using a contract or writing proposal worksheets or calculating your costs. Because if you were, you would know to the penny what your parties are costing you. Instead I'd guess that clients call you and you are so glad to get the business that you say yes right away and start purchasing food, props, and equipment immediately. You never get deposit money or discuss the terms of who is paying for what. You just assume it will all be fine. Am I right?

Shortcuts can make you miss the most important parts of the deal. Start fresh today. Create a contract checklist and keep it next to the phone. The next time a client calls, start from the top. Don't promise or quote a price until you have worked the calculator. Don't undersell your talent or your product.

If you go through the process we have discussed in this book, you can't help but make money.

Question Twelve

I'm making good money in my business but I only get calls from clients who never want to spend much. What can I do?

Change your attitude and expand your horizon. Look to target wealthier and more sophisticated clients. This is a marketing and image problem. I am a firm believer that you attract the clientele you deserve. That may be blunt and I'm sorry, but try to figure out whether your approach is at fault.

I look to competition I admire when I am trying to solve my problems. How are they getting clientele? What do their brochures or ads say? Maybe I can follow some of their steps without spending a lot of money.

Contact your chamber of commerce and find out if they have mailing lists available that target professional organizations. You know who is making the most money in your area. Who is providing services for them now?

Be sure not to make excuses for yourself. Get beyond the excuse stage and go after the clients you want.

Appendix

Culinary Schooling/Education

California Culinary Academy
625 Polk Street
San Francisco, CA 94102
(800) BAY-CHEF

Catering courses at the California Culinary Academy (CCA) run
throughout the sixteen months of the Chef's Program. They also
offer continuing education courses.

The Culinary Institute of America
443 Albany Post Road
Hyde Park, NY 12538
(914) 452–9430

The Culinary Institute of America offers a five-day catering
course through its continuing-education department.

The French Culinary Institute
462 Broadway
New York, NY 10013
(212) 219–8890

For serious French cuisine aficionados, The French Culinary Institute offers a 600-hour professional training course. No specific courses are offered for catering at this time.

Johnson and Wales University
Culinary Arts Division
1 Washington Avenue
Providence, RI 02905
(401) 456–1130

Johnson and Wales University is a prestigious cooking school, highly recommended for the professional chef. Special courses include Catering/Garde-Manager (presentation of cold foods), and Catering Management.

The New England Culinary Institute
250 Main Street
Montpelier, VT 05602
(802) 223–6324

The New England Culinary Institute offers some catering instruction in the two-year program.

The New York Restaurant School
27 West Thirty-fourth Street
New York, NY 10001
(212) 947–7097

The New York Restaurant School does not offer catering courses, but it does have apprenticeships available with caterers who attend the twenty-week Culinary Arts Program.

Peter Kump's New York Cooking School
307 East Ninety-second Street
New York, NY 10128
(212) 410–4601

The business of catering and cooking for catering services is offered twice a year at Peter Kump's New York Cooking School. Both courses last five days and are available for the beginner and intermediate caterer.

Scottsdale Culinary Institute
8100 East Camelback Road
Scottsdale, AZ 85251
(602) 990–3773

Banquet and catering classes are offered at the Scottsdale Culinary Institute's forty-week curriculum. It also has continuing-education courses on catering.

UCLA/Extension Services
Culinary and Food Service Department, Room 514
10995 Le Conte Avenue
Los Angeles, CA 90024
(310) 206–8120

The University of California at Los Angeles offers excellent courses designed for individuals looking to enter the catering profession. Instructors are working professionals from the community and graduates of the CCA or CIA.

Western Culinary Institute
1316 Southwest Thirteenth Avenue
Portland, OR 97201
(503) 223–2245 or (800) 666–0312

The Western Culinary Institute offers a twelve-month Diploma Program of extensive hands-on training for those wanting a culinary career. The regular curriculum covers banquet work. At this time it does not offer an individual course in catering.

Westlake Culinary Institute
4643 Lake View Canyon Road
Westlake Village, CA 91361
(818) 991–3940

The Westlake Culinary Institute offers a three-weekend catering series, taught twice a year. Certificates are awarded upon completion.

Recommended Reading

An excellent reference book for cooking schools around the world is *The Guide to Cooking Schools* by Doris Shaw. You can order this directly by calling Book Passage in Corte Madera, California, at their toll-free number: (800) 321–9785, or by writing to Shaw Associates, Publishers, 625 Biltmore Way, Suite 1406, Coral Gables, FL 33134 (305–446–8888).

Along with the collection of cookbooks I know you already own, consider the following when you've got money to invest in your education:

Books from the heart that will inspire you to cook

The Art of Eating, M. F. K. Fisher (Macmillan, 1990)
An Omelette and a Glass of Wine, Elizabeth David (Penguin Books, 1986)

Book that will impress your clients

Larousse Gastronomique, Jennifer Harvey Lang (Crown Books, 1988)

Books that will teach you to cook

Jacques Pepin's La Technique (Random House, 1976)
Jacques Pepin's La Methode (Random House, 1979)
The Joy of Cooking, Vols. 1 and 2, Irma S. Rombauer and Marion Rombauer Becker (NAL-Dutton, 1974)
Mastering the Art of French Cooking, Julia Child (Knopf, 1983)
The Way to Cook, Julia Child (Knopf, 1989)
Anne Willan's Look and Cook series; 24 volumes (Dorling Kindersley, 1992)

Books with beautiful pictures and presentations

The Best of Gourmet, Gourmet Magazine (Random House, 1991, 1992)
Entertaining, Martha Stewart, (Potter, 1982)
The Natural Cuisine of Georges Blanc (Stewart, Tabori and Chang, 1987)
Pacific Flavors, Hugh Carpenter (Stewart, Tabori and Chang, 1988, 1993)

Books that you should buy when you are a student

Kitchen Science, Howard Hillman (Houghton Mifflin, 1989)
The New Professional Chef, Culinary Institute of America (VNR, 1991)
On Food and Cooking, Harold McGee (Macmillan, 1984)
The Professional Caterers Series, Vols. 1–4, Denis Ruffel (VNR, 1990)
Professional Cooking, Wayne Gisslen (Wiley, 1989)
Successful Buffet Management, Ronald Yudd (VNR, 1989)

Books to buy if the bakery is closed

The Cake Bible, Rose Levy Berenbaum (Morrow, 1988)
The Italian Baker, Carol Field (Harper Collins, 1985)
The Professional Pastry Chef, Bo Friberg (VNR, 1990)

Industry magazines

Fancy Foods
Talcott Publishing
206 West Huron Street
Chicago, IL 60610
(312) 664–4040

A good magazine to consult if you want to learn about new products on the market.

Food Arts: The Magazine for Professionals
Food Arts Publishing, Inc.
M. Shanken, Publishers
387 Park Avenue South
New York, NY 10016
(212) 684–4224

Food Arts is an up-to-date voice of the food industry today addressing restaurants and caterers.

Special Events Magazine
Miramar Publishing
P.O. Box 3640
Culver City, CA 90231–3640
(800) 543–4116

Special Events Magazine covers current party trends and offers informative articles about how industry professionals create their spectacular parties.

Bookstores catering to cooks

The Cook's Library
8373 West Third Street
Los Angeles, CA 90048
(213) 655–3141

Kitchen Art and Letters
1435 Lexington Avenue
New York, NY 10128
(212) 876–5550

Both these bookstores take a serious interest in providing the most current and recommended reading on cooking. If one of these two bookstores doesn't have the book you want, chances are you don't need it!

Trade Shows

Throughout the year trade shows are held in cities all over the country at which vendors in our industry introduce their products. As a professional, attending these trade shows gives you an opportunity to research, sample, and update your knowledge of equipment and services. Along with miles of purveyors' booths, many of the shows also present keynote speakers in a relaxed and informal setting.

Check with your local convention center about upcoming trade shows affiliated with the hospitality industry. To purchase a general admission ticket requires only a business name and a business card. The following is a list of the most prestigious trade shows held every year. Registration fees usually run from $10 to $30.

Fancy Food Show
National Association for the Specialty Food Trade, Inc.
8 West Fortieth Street, Fourth Floor
New York, NY 10018
Convention information number: (800) 255–2502

Also billed as the International Confectionary Show, this trade show is held every six months in either San Francisco, San Diego, or New York. Exhibitors from all over the world are on hand to introduce their products. This trade show is basically geared to chocolates, cookies, biscuits, and nuts.

The National Restaurant Association Hotel-Motel Show
150 North Michigan Avenue, Suite 2000
Chicago, IL 60601
Convention information number: (800) 424–5156

About 100,000 people from all over the United States and Europe attend this trade show, held at McCormick Place in Chicago every May. The kitchens built here are specifically designed to house the final tryouts for the U.S. Culinary Team in "The Food Olympics." It is imperative to reserve a hotel room early. Complimentary shuttle buses from most of the major hotels are provided to and from McCormick Center throughout the show.

Special Events Magazine Industry Conference
P.O. Box 3640
Culver City, CA 90231–3640
Convention information number: (800) 637–5995

Each January *Special Events Magazine* creates the industry's first and foremost convention. This successful conference has been held in San Diego, New Orleans, and Orlando, Florida. Seminars are available on catering, decor, and successful business ideas for the nineties.

Professional Organizations

Join as many professional organizations in your area as possible. They're a wonderful way for you to meet other caterers, food writers, and a host of other professionals involved in the food-service industry. Many of them also offer classes and other benefits.

American Culinary Foundation
P.O. Box 3466
St. Augustine, FL 32085
(904) 824–4468

Industry experience can earn you accrediatation in this organization.

American Institute of Wine and Food
1550 Bryant Street
San Francisco, CA 94103
(415) 255–3000

This national, nonprofit group was founded by Julia Child,
Robert Mondavi, and other professionals. Monthly meetings are
dedicated to the appreciation of exquisite food and excellent
wine. Check to see whether your city has a chapter. Participate
in the group's fund-raisers, and you'll have a chance to rub
shoulders with seasoned professionals, who may recommend
you for jobs.

International Association of Cooking Professionals
304 West Liberty Street, Suite 301
Louisville, KY 40202
(502) 583–3783

A national networking group of chefs, stylists, cooking instructors, and writers.

The National Restaurant Association
1200 Seventeenth Street, Northwest
Washington, D.C. 20036
(800) 424–5156

By joining this national organization, you can be assured that
you will be up to date on state and federal legislation pertaining
to the hospitality industry. The national association maintains a
resource library for members and can refer them to state restaurant associations, many of which offer classes on food safety
and other subjects at state restaurant shows in conjunction with
the Educational Foundation of the NRA.

Index

W

wait staff, in pricing, 87
wholesale food purveyors,
    31–32
word-processing software,
    135–36
workers' compensation insur-
    ance, 57

Y

Yellow Pages, 46, 119
    information for ad, 107

About the Author

Denise Vivaldo, a professionally trained chef, is the owner of Food Fanatics, a food styling and consulting firm. She specializes in international recipes, menu development, staff training, and exceptional food presentation. She lives in Los Angeles with her adorable husband and two big dogs.